The Conquistador 1492–1550

John Pohl • Illustrated by Adam Hook

First published in Great Britain in 2001 by Osprey Publishing, Elms Court, Chapel Way, Botley, Oxford OX2 9LP, United Kingdom.
Email: info@ospreypublishing.com

ISBN 1 84176 175 3

Editor: Nikolai Bogdanovic
Design: Ken Vail Graphic Design, Cambridge, UK
Index by Alison Worthington
Originated by Magnet Harlequin, Uxbridge, UK
Printed in China through World Print Ltd.

01 02 03 04 05   10 9 8 7 6 5 4 3 2 1

FOR A CATALOG OF ALL BOOKS PUBLISHED BY OSPREY MILITARY AND AVIATION PLEASE CONTACT:

The Marketing Manager, Osprey Direct USA,
c/o Motorbooks International, PO Box 1,
Osceola, WI 54020-0001, USA.
Email: info@ospreydirectusa.com

The Marketing Manager, Osprey Direct UK, PO Box 140,
Wellingborough, Northants, NN8 4ZA, United Kingdom.
Email: info@ospreydirect.co.uk

www.ospreypublishing.com

Artist's note

Readers may care to note that the original paintings from which the color plates in this book were prepared are available for private sale. All reproduction copyright whatsoever is retained by the Publishers. All enquiries should be addressed to:

Scorpio Gallery, PO Box 475, Hailsham, East Sussex, BN27 2SL, UK.

The Publishers regret that they can enter into no correspondence upon this matter.

FRONT COVER **The Conquistador Pedro de Alvarado, known by the Aztecs as Tonatiuh, campaigning in Guatemala in 1523. (The *Lienzo de Tlaxcala*)**

CONTENTS

THE CONQUISTADOR 1492–1550

INTRODUCTION – THE BATTLE OF CENTLA 1519

Miguel de la Cruz was nervous as he slogged forward through the mud of the canal. Cortés had just led the cavalry away into the dense underbrush to find ground more suitable for horse, which left the foot soldiers dangerously exposed to a direct attack by no fewer than 8,000 Mayas who had gathered on the open field up ahead. If only the old friars back in Trujillo knew just how frightening their tales of a devil's army could truly be. Ferocious in their appearance, many of the Mayas wore helmets carved in the shapes of jaguars and other fantastic creatures; the array of shimmering plumes and banners that they carried was electrifying in the blazing sun. Miguel had fought Indian people before, but this army seemed more like some terrible legion of ancient myth. As the enemy's drums and conch shell trumpets began to sound, Diego de Ordás signaled to his men to prepare for the attack. Miguel blew on the fuse of his matchlock confidently. Soon the frightening cries of the enemy began to grow louder. Miguel raised his weapon and took aim counting out the distance in his mind. Just a few more seconds, 'Fire!' cried Ordás. Miguel pushed the button trigger, the fuse sprung into the pan, and the heavy gun lurched backward with an ear-shattering blast. The gunner stepped sideways to reload, allowing a swordsman to take his place. Suddenly a Maya warrior, badly shot and covered in blood, shrieked through the thick curtain of smoke swinging his *macuahuitl*, a vicious wooden club edged with volcanic glass razors. The swordsman immediately brought the Indian man to his knees with a single thrust through the chest. The Maya fell, rolled over, and gasped. Miguel stared in disbelief at his good fortune and tore the golden bracelet from

One of the more romantic interpretations of Columbus – there are no confirmed portraits from life. Ignorant, blundering, vain and avaricious, Columbus set the disastrous and irreversible course of Spanish military policy in the Caribbean. (Engraving published by Théodore DeBry, 1591)

the dead man's wrist. Miguel was a proud Spaniard, devoted to his god and the Holy Roman Emperor Carlos V. Now, fingering the ornament, he hoped to become a very rich man ... if he could just survive long enough.

Forty years earlier, King Ferdinand and Queen Isabel had joined the Iberian kingdoms of Aragon and Castile to begin a course of Spanish expansion that would lead to the defeat of the Islamic Emirate of Granada, the discovery of the Americas, and the invasion of Italy. In 1492, Columbus returned from Española (Haiti-Santo Domingo) with reports of new lands populated by an indigenous people who possessed no metal tools or weapons but a great deal of gold. In 1493 he established a colony of 1,500 men, but he was unable to deal with divisive factions among both the Spanish colonists and the Arawak Indian people. Open revolts ensued that led to the ruthless military subjugation of the island of Española, only concluding with Columbus' own arrest. Succeeding administrators were hardly more competent and just as murderous. Under Friar Nicolás de Ovando, Anacoana, the wife of a paramount Arawak chief was hanged, and other rebellious leaders were burned alive. Ovando then instituted the *encomienda* system by which large numbers of the Indian population were condemned to work in permanent servitude to Spanish landowners. In 1509, Columbus' son, Diego, was appointed governor. Unable to control the ambitions of wealthy landowners like Ponce de León, Esquivel, Narváez and Velásquez, the first Conquistadors overran Puerto Rico, Jamaica, and Cuba in three short years, killing anyone and anything that got in the way of their search for gold.

For years Muslim princes had paid tribute in the precious yellow metal and fashioned magnificent objects of art and ornamentation from it. But by the 15th century European monarchs wanted to emulate the Florentines and produce gold coinage. Gold soon began to haunt the imagination of Spaniards as the one commodity that could transcend the oppressive limitations of social rank. Columbus bluntly stated that a man with enough gold could even take souls to paradise. Yet by 1519, the Spanish Main was a pitiful shell of its former prosperity. Most of the gold placers had been worked out, and the Arawak Indian people, the real wealth of the land, had been mercilessly exploited on plantations and ranches. Disease was rampant, reducing the Arawak population of Española alone from one million in 1492 to less than 16,000 in 1518. Men like Miguel, who had sailed to the New World in search of prosperity, became desperate; they felt they had little alternative but to turn to what they knew best – killing for a living.

Small gold ornaments of a style traded widely between Central America, the Caribbean, and South America. Some of the gold that Columbus obtained was smelted with copper to give it a richer color. Called *guanín,* the metal led to accusations that he was attempting to cheat the crown. Cortés later told Indian lords that the Spaniards suffered from a disease that only gold could cure. (Private collection)

5

Many of the Conquistadors and their men came from Extremadura in western Spain, including Cortés, Alvarado, and Pizarro. The region was characterized by broad stretches of open, rocky, grassland. More conducive to cattle-raising than farming, peasant youths would eventually take their chances in the army after droughts devastated the area in the early 1500s. (Photo by Richard Diehl)

At the battle of Centla, the shower of arrows and stones fell like black rain over the Spaniards. After an hour of hard fighting, the Mayas had withdrawn from hand-to-hand combat, hoping to beat down their enemy with missile fire. Sixty of the 300 infantry had been wounded, several had limbs nearly severed by the vicious *macuahuitl*. Miguel himself had been badly injured by a sling stone to his shoulder. Cortés and the cavalry had still not appeared and the situation was beginning to look desperate. Then a glint of metal flashed in Miguel's eyes and he squinted through the smoke and sun to see a man on a gray horse swinging his sword in the air. 'Santiago!' cried the men in the front of the line – Saint James, the patron saint of Spain. Every Conquistador knew his image emblazoned on the flags they carried into battle. Could it truly be that he now appeared so miraculously in such a strange land? Suddenly the earth began to tremble with a fearful sound that the Spaniards knew well. Cortés, Alvarado, and the rest of the cavalry came riding down the Maya columns slashing and lancing men to death on all sides. The Indians were terrified by the giants who seemed to be half-men and half-deer. Despite the efforts of their captains to hold their formations, they broke into a mass of confusion and fled into the jungle. Cortés turned and rode up to the foot soldiers demanding to know what all the chatter was about. Ordás explained that the men had taken Francisco de Morla to be none other than Santiago himself, here to drive off their enemies. Cortés looked at Morla sitting astride his dapple gray and the two burst out laughing. Miguel didn't really know whether or not he had witnessed a miracle, but he dropped to his knees and began to pray for his salvation all the same.

CHRONOLOGY – PRINCIPAL EVENTS AND CAMPAIGNS 1479–1532

Typical men-at-arms as they might have appeared during the Spanish Reconquista and early Renaissance wars in Italy. Their armor, dress, and equipment is similar to that available to Conquistador armies. (19th century illustration by Carl Häberlin)

1479 Ferdinand of Aragon and Isabel of Castile are married, uniting much of central and eastern Spain.

1484 Birth of Hernán Cortés.

1491–92 Ferdinand and Isabel defeat the Moors under Muhammad XI Boabdil at Granada. Columbus, together with Vicente Yáñez Pinzón and his brother Martín Alonso, land at Española. The Spaniards form an alliance with the Arawak chief Guacanagari and found the town of La Natividad on the island's northwestern coast.

1493 Maximilian Habsburg becomes Holy Roman Emperor as Maximilian I.

1493–96 Columbus makes a second voyage to Española. He finds La Natividad has been destroyed, the colonists having been put to death by a hostile faction of Arawaks. The Spaniards found a second community at La Isabela 60 miles to the east. The colony is beset by hurricanes, epidemics, and fire. Open warfare again breaks out with the Arawaks over demands for labor and tribute in gold. Columbus' brother Bartholomew founds Santo Domingo on the southern coast. Huayna Capac becomes emperor of the Inca Empire.

1495 Ferdinand and Isabel dispatch an army to defend Aragon's claims to Sicily and southern Italy against France's Charles VIII. For the next ten years, the Spaniards under such remarkable commanders as Gonzalo Fernández de Córdoba participate in wars between the French, the Holy Roman Empire, the Pope, and the Italian city states.

1497 Francisco Roldán leads an insurrection against Columbus. His faction of La Isabela colonists move west to ally themselves with an Arawak faction under paramount chief Behechio and his sister Anacoana.

1498–1500 Columbus makes a third voyage of exploration to South America. He is returned to Spain in chains after being accused of administrative incompetence and corruption.

1499–1500 Vicente Yañez Pinzón carries out slave raids along the north coast of Columbia, confirming the existence of the South American continent.

1502–04 Columbus embarks on a fourth and final voyage of exploration following the coast of Honduras, Nicaragua, Costa Rica and Panama. He encounters Indian canoe traffic in rich luxury goods providing first evidence of the tremendous wealth of Mesoamerican civilizations. Motecuhzoma II is elected Aztec emperor at age 34.

1503 Gonzalo de Córdoba defeats the Marquis di Saluzzo at the battle of Garigliano forcing the French to withdraw from Italy. Battle-hardened veterans return to Spain where they learn of the new-found wealth of the 'Indies.' Some, including the future Conquistador of Peru, Francisco de Pizarro, are encouraged to redirect their military talents to the invasion of the western hemisphere. Operating under orders from Nicolás de Ovando, the governor of Santo Domingo in Española, Diego de Velásquez executes Anacoana and 80 subordinate chiefs, completing the subjugation of western Española.

1504 Queen Isabel dies. Juan de Esquivel and Juan Ponce de León conquer eastern Española and the island is made a Spanish colony. Plantations and ranches replace gold-mining as the primary economic ventures. Increased demand for slave labor to work the land fosters further expansion throughout the Caribbean.

1504–06 Juan de la Cosa, Alonso de Hojeda, Diego de Nicuesa and others attempt to establish settlements on the mainland of Central and South America with variable success. Abandoned by Hojeda, Francisco de Pizarro establishes a settlement at Urabá, Colombia. Hostilities with local chiefs subsequently force the Spaniards to relocate to Darién.

1506 Columbus dies. Hernan Cortés embarks from Spain for Española.

1508 Vicente Yáñez Pinzón and Juan Díaz de Solis explore the coast of Honduras and the Yucatan Peninsula confirming the existence of Mesoamerica to the east.

1509 Ponce de León subdues Puerto Rico. Juan de Esquivel and Pánfilo de Narváez conquer Jamaica.

A woodcut illustrates Protestants, Moors, and Jews being burned alive. During the late 15th century, Ferdinand and Isabel attempted to forge a new Spanish national identity by persecuting all non-Catholics. This ruthless policy of self-righteousness and intolerance was enacted with the same zeal by their representatives in the western hemisphere and had an equally devastating effect on its indigenous peoples. (Author's illustration)

1511 Traveling from Darien to Española, Gonzalo Guerrero and Geronimo de Aguilar are shipwrecked on the Yucatan Peninsula. Guerrero eventually becomes a Maya warlord and leads troops against the Spaniards in many subsequent battles. Aguilar becomes Cortés' translator after he is rescued in 1519.

1512–14 Diego Velásquez de Cuellar and Pánfilo de Narváez conquer Cuba. Cortés participates, gaining invaluable knowledge of how to conduct campaigns against Indian armies. Velásquez is appointed governor. Cortés serves as his secretary and later gains wealth through cattle and gold enterprises.

1513 On a mission to locate new sources of gold, pearls, and slaves, Vasco Nuñez de Balboa crosses the Isthmus of Panama thereby opening up the Pacific coast to Spanish expansionism. Pizarro participates in the expedition. Ponce de León explores Florida.

1515 Francis I becomes king of France and initiates new campaigns in Italy. Spain engages in ten years of nearly continuous warfare on the Italian peninsula.

1516 Ferdinand dies. His daughter's son, Charles, succeeds him as the first king of a united Spain. Three years later, Charles is elected Holy Roman Emperor as Charles V upon the death of his paternal grandfather Maximilian I.

1517 Acting on reports of rich lands to the east, Governor Velásquez sends Córdoba to explore the Yucatan Peninsula. He returns only after suffering numerous casualties at the hands of the Chontal, and dies of wounds shortly after.

1518 Encouraged by reports of vast populations living in cities, Velásquez sends a second expedition under Juan de Grijalva. Lacking the necessary supplies to carry out any protracted campaign along the coast of Yucatan or Tabasco, Grijalva reaches Veracruz and decides to return to Cuba.

1519 Velásquez sends Cortés on a third expedition to Mexico. He traverses the Gulf coast and eventually lands at Veracruz where he allies himself with the Totonacs. He founds the settlement of Villa Rica. In September, allied with the Tlaxcalteca, he enters Tenochtitlan and seizes Motecuhzoma as a hostage. The city of Panama is founded. Magellan embarks on a three-year voyage around the world. Nuñez de Balboa is beheaded for treason in Panama.

1520 Velásquez sends Narváez to arrest Cortés in April. Cortés defeats Narváez and returns to Tenochtitlan reinforced with his men and supplies. Pedro de Alvarado massacres the Aztec nobility at the festival of Toxcatl. Motecuhzoma is killed and the Spaniards are forced to flee Tenochtitlan. Recovering from near total annihilation, Cortés rebuilds his army in Tlaxcala. Smallpox spreads through Mexico from the Spanish settlement at Veracruz.

1521 Cortés besieges Tenochtitlan with an army of over 900 Spaniards and ultimately more than 50,000 Indian allies. After eight months of continuous fighting, Tenochtitlan surrenders, bringing an end to the most powerful Indian empire in North America. Ponce de León dies of wounds after his second expedition to Florida.

1522–23 Cortés leads an expedition into West Mexico. Pedro de Alvarado, Cortés' former second-in-command, attacks the city-states of Mixtec and Zapotec in Oaxaca, then embarks on a campaign against the highland Maya of Guatemala. He ceases hostilities upon confronting a formidable Pipil army in El Salvador.

A commemorative medal bears a portrait of Cortés in 1529. Cortés was described as having pale skin and brown hair with a reddish hue. The artist may have intended to portray a scar crossing over the cheek. Cortés was known to have suffered severe head wounds during his campaigns. (Author's illustration)

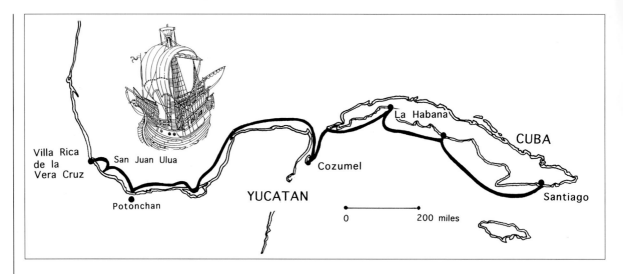

1524–26 Velásquez dies. Cortés embarks on a punitive expedition after Cristóbal de Olid in Honduras and traverses Guatemala's Petén jungle. The last Aztec emperor, Cuauhtémoc, is taken along as hostage, but is executed. Francisco Pizarro leads an expedition south into Colombia. Spanish and Imperial troops defeat the French at the battle of Pavia, Italy.

1526–27 Pizarro makes a second expedition, sailing as far south as Ecuador where he trades for gold, llamas, and other luxury goods, tangible proof of the existence of a vast Inca empire in Peru. Inca Emperor Huayna Capac dies of smallpox. His sons, Atahualpa and Huascar, dispute the inheritance to the Incan empire. Francisco de Montejo initiates his campaign against the Maya of the Yucatan Peninsula.

1528 Cortés returns to Spain where both he and Pizarro meet with Emperor Charles. Cortés is appointed Marquis of the Valley of Oaxaca. Pizarro is commissioned to invade the Incan empire. Succeeding Velásquez as governor of Cuba, Narváez leads a doomed expedition to Florida. An officer named Cabeza de Vaca is among a handful of survivors who reach Mexico after ten years of Indian captivity and wandering. His report inspires both the de Soto and Coronado expeditions.

1529–30 Nuño de Guzmán subjugates West Mexico. The Treaty of Cambrai concludes hostilities between France, Spain, Italy, and the Holy Roman Empire in Europe.

1531–35 Pizarro leads an army of 160 men into Peru. Hernando de Soto serves as cavalry commander. Upon hearing that Atahualpa is marching south to crown himself emperor in Cuzco, Pizarro intercepts the monarch and executes him. The Spaniards then embark on an 800-mile campaign, fighting their way into the Inca capital where they govern for two years through Huayna Capac's son, Manco. Lima is later founded as the new Spanish capital of Peru. Cortés leads an expedition to the Gulf of California. Francisco de Montejo campaigns in Tabasco and Campeche.

1539–42 Hernando de Soto leaves Cuba, invades Florida, then moves north and east making war on largely Muskogean Indian nations from Georgia to Louisiana until he dies from fever. Luis de Moscoso assumes command of the expedition and flees to Veracruz. Juan Rodriguez Cabrillo explores the Pacific coast of California and Oregon.

1540–42 Francisco Vásquez de Coronado invades the southwestern United States. He wages campaigns against the Zuni and Rio Grande Pueblo Indian peoples among others until he realizes there is little fortune to be gained and returns to Mexico.

1541 Pedro de Alvarado dies of wounds near Guadalajara, Mexico. Pizarro is assassinated at Lima, Peru.

1547 Cortés dies at Castilleja de la Cuesta outside Seville, Spain.

Map illustrating Cortés' route from Cuba to Veracruz. Cortés was tactically prepared for what he would encounter because many of his men had participated in the two previous expeditions along the same coastline under Córdoba in 1517, and Grijalva in 1518. (Author's illustration)

RECRUITMENT AND MOBILIZATION

Miguel had no wealth, nor did he come from a prominent family like some of the Conquistador leaders such as Cortés, Alvarado, or Ordás. A veteran of the Italian wars which were largely financed by Caribbean wealth, Miguel had returned to his dry desolate homeland of Extremadura in southwestern Spain only to find that his family had been driven off their farms when the fields were turned over to sheep and cattle-grazing. A simple desire for freedom from poverty and obligations to petty lords and bishops was all the motivation Miguel needed. He had just enough money to take him to the Caribbean.

Men traveling aboard 16th century ships equated the experience with six weeks of torture. They were confined in narrow holds below deck most of the time, where the stench of spoiled food, vomit, animals, and manure was overpowering. Yet somehow they managed by gambling, singing, dancing – anything that would keep their minds off their torment. Miguel and his contemporaries were fond of the ballads of great heroes like Charlemagne, Roland and especially, El Cid, the 11th century Iberian conqueror. Books were becoming more commonplace and the ship's captain possessed a copy of *Amadís de Gaula*. The men sat for hours listening to the adventures of mythical heroes like Gasquilan and his shield of gold. The stories made such a profound impression on the Spaniards that they eventually named many lands they discovered after the fabled kingdoms of their novels: Amazon, California, and Patagonia. The name for the islands of the 'Antilles' was even derived from the legend of the lost city of Atlantis itself. Some said that the sagas were nonsense, but there were legends of

Sailors like these drawn in 1529 were invaluable to Conquistador armies. They not only guided the ships through unknown waters in all sorts of formidable weather conditions, but served as engineers on land. Most were of Portuguese, Genoese, and Neapolitan descent.
(Weiditz, 1927)

great epochs of gold and silver dating before the fall of Adam and Eve. Surely, these lost worlds had some basis in fact; it was just a question of going in search of them.

When Miguel arrived at Española, the colonists were excited by the latest news of a mainland located to the west. Since 1502 successive explorations along the coasts of Colombia, Panama, Honduras, the Yucatan Peninsula, and Florida seemed to confirm the existence of a vast land mass. In 1517, Velásquez, the lieutenant-governor of Cuba, financed a slaving expedition under the command of Fernández de Córdoba. Córdoba attempted to land in Tabasco but was attacked by the Maya. His men were nearly annihilated and he himself later died of wounds. However, reports of societies of people living in great cities convinced Velásquez to finance a trading expedition under his nephew, Juan de Grijalva, the following year. Like Córdoba, Grijalva also encountered strong resistance to landings within Maya territory, but found willing trading partners further north among both the Aztec and Totonac peoples of Veracruz. It soon became clear that there were divisive factions at work in mainland Indian politics, an observation that Cortés later noted and exploited.

Grijalva sent one of his captains, Pedro de Alvarado, back to Cuba with men wounded during the expedition. There he displayed what amounted to between 16,000 and 20,000 pesos of gold the expedition had acquired. It was enough to convince Velásquez that a well-supplied military expedition could turn a substantial profit. But loyal as Grijalva had been, Alvarado convinced Velásquez that his nephew was incompetent and that he should appoint someone else to command. Velásquez decided to appoint Hernando Cortés 'caudillo' or captain of the new expedition.

Miguel knew that Cortés would need gunners and so he continued on board ship to Santiago de Cuba where he presented himself. A soldier's life depended on an experienced commander, and there seemed to be very few on the early Spanish Main. Miguel learned that Cortés had been born in Extremadura at Medellin in 1485. He was the son of a *hidalgo*, a rank of minor nobility, but the family was hardly rich, earning most of their income from farming and rents. Cortés was sent to Salamanca for his education. His parents had hoped that he would pursue a career in law, but although he was a competent student, he excelled at arms. When he returned to Medellin, Cortés vacillated between joining a command under the great captain Gonzalo Fernández de Córdoba who was organizing an army to fight the French in Italy, or seeking his fortune in the Caribbean. Convinced that greater wealth lay with the latter, he embarked, aged 22, for Española. Having

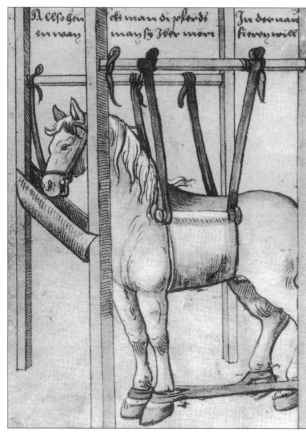

The question of how to transport horses aboard ship was resolved with an ingenious system of hoists, harnesses, and slings to restrain the animals on deck. At 3,000 pesos each, horses were expensive but absolutely crucial to Conquistador campaigns. (Weiditz, 1927)

The Spaniards were the first to employ what would later become known as 'battleship diplomacy' in their dealings with foreign nations. Faced with increasing dissent among a faction of men loyal to Velásquez, Cortés had his ships scuttled shortly after arriving at Veracruz, thereby making the entire army solely dependent on his command. (Detail from an engraving published by Théodore DeBry, 1591)

participated in the persecution of the Arawaks following the death of Anacoana, Cortés came to the attention of Velásquez and was invited to join him during his invasion of Cuba. Here Cortés would learn that absolute brutality paid absolutely, as he witnessed Velásquez slaughter and enslave an entire Indian population in a matter of months.

Cortés proved to be a resourceful adjutant and was appointed secretary of the new colony. Although political disputes subsequently divided the men, Velásquez knew that Cortés had profited from his mining and ranching enterprises to such an extent that he could personally afford to invest heavily in an expedition. In 1519, Velásquez drafted a contract listing Cortés' responsibilities for a forthcoming expedition to Mexico. This being an expedition above all to serve God, blasphemy, gambling, and sleeping with women were, of course, expressly prohibited. The fleet was to keep together and travel west along the coast following the route of Grijalva. All Indian populations that they encountered were to be informed of the power of the king of Spain and his demand that they place themselves under his protective authority. A treasurer and inspector were to be appointed to collect and record all objects of precious metals and stones. Landings were only permitted for the purpose of gathering wood, food, and water. Cortés was to discover the nature of gold sources especially in the Totonac area of Veracruz and to determine the truth of reports of Amazons and half-human creatures. To these instructions Cortés had been careful to add an escape clause, which gave him powers to carry out actions not detailed in the contract, and to act as a legal authority.

Miguel was satisfied with his terms of employment and was shown to a house where he could stay with other soldiers until the expedition got under way. While he awaited the governor's final permission, Cortés had succeeded in recruiting 300 men by advertising the expedition via Santiago's town crier. Within two weeks of his appointment he had

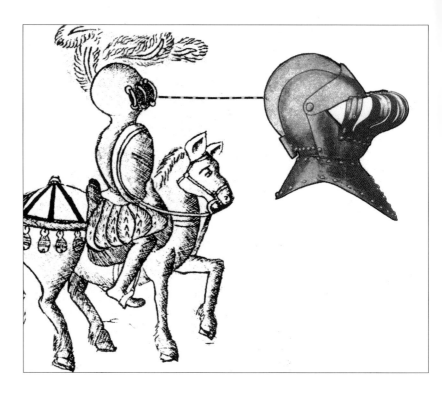

The stereotype of the Conquistador is of a mounted knight in full armor. Although painted by Indian people who had considerable knowledge of events, such images are more likely derived from religious pageants that were celebrated in Spanish Colonial times to glorify the Conquistadors. For example, note that this horseman from Sahagún's *Florentine Codex* is wearing a 'caged' burgonet, a late 16th century helmet style that was only displayed at special ceremonies of state and never worn in battle. (Author's illustration)

assembled sufficient arms, artillery, and munitions on credit. Weavers were even commissioned to fabricate cotton Indian-style jackets of quilted armor. Cortés purchased a caravel and a brigantine which, with Alvarado's ship, brought the total to three. Four more would join him shortly.

In the meantime, Grijalva had returned from Veracruz. His report largely cleared his name of Alvarado's slander and now Velásquez was having serious doubts about Cortés. Cortés was quick to learn of his partner's change of heart and immediately prepared to set sail. Velásquez only heard of Cortés' intentions when the town butcher came to inform him that he had been stripped of two weeks' supply of meat. 'How is this, compadre, that you are now setting off?' called Velásquez from the quay. Cortés was already in a boat heading for his flagship. He merely shouted back that everything was going according to plan and directed his men to set sail.

Nevertheless, the expedition was still short of food, men, and supplies. Cortés stopped at Pilón on Cape Cruz and received 1,000 rations of cassava bread from a friend with a plantation in the area. He also directed one of his ships to sail to Jamaica to acquire 800 sides of bacon in addition to 2,000 more rations of bread. Next, the army landed further west at Trinidad where the local magistrate had been instructed to detain Cortés and remove him as commander. Cortés met with his officers and by invoking autonomous powers in his contract, persuaded them to allow him to retain command. One of his lieutenants, Ordás, proved his loyalty by immediately seizing a passing ship that was loaded with supplies for the colony of Darien in Panama, a bold act that could be taken for piracy. By now 200 more soldiers had joined the expedition; many had just returned with Grijalva and recognized the potential of this operation proposed by a more aggressive commander.

Horses were obtained from the magistrate of Trinidad who ignored Velásquez's orders to arrest Cortés, doubtless on a promise of a share in profits. Descendants of those originally brought from Spain by Columbus, these horses could cost as much as 3,000 pesos each. They were short-legged, but sturdy enough to carry a man in armor on a heavy Moorish saddle. Dogs were also recruited. Wolf hounds or mastiffs had proved effective in battle since medieval times, and packs were particularly useful in combat against indigenous light infantry. Finally, and perhaps most important to the diplomatic success of the expedition, were large quantities of glass beads, bells, mirrors, needles, and pins, as well as iron knives, scissors, tongs, hammers, and axes – objects that had become commonplace in European societies since Roman times but were unheard of in Mesoamerica. Gift-giving was the primary form of aristocratic social exchange among the civilizations of Mexico. Glass was unknown and so simple beads became priceless in an economy where they had never previously existed; furthermore their possession became the mark of those who had access to new trading partners and exotic forms of commerce in general. Although metallurgy had been adopted from South America by AD 900, it was practiced by royal craft specialists for the production of gold, silver, copper jewelry and other prized commodities. The iron objects that the Spaniards introduced were regarded with much the same sense of exotic value and fascination.

Perhaps dating to the late 1520s, a manuscript preserved in the Benson library at the University of Texas, Austin, may be the earliest indigenous portrayal of Cortés' army on the march to Tlaxcala by eyewitnesses. Note that the men are wearing late medieval to early Renaissance dress and little or no armor. (Author's illustration)

By February 1519, enough water, bread, smoked meat, salt, oil, vinegar, and wine had been loaded to last 500 men the few weeks it would take to reconnoiter the coastline from Yucatan to Veracruz, after which the expedition expected to survive on local resources through trade or seizure. Veterans of the previous expeditions recommended loading as many barrels of water as possible, as supplies were frequently unpredictable and could be defended by hostile communities. Cortés needed to ensure that he could feed and water his men on his own terms and not become subject to the desperate acts of starvation and thirst that had endangered the Córdoba and Grijalva expeditions.

Despite being separated during the first night, all but one of the ships made the 50 miles between Cuba and the Yucatan Peninsula without incident. Landing at Cozumel, the Spaniards were welcomed by apprehensive Mayas. Ten days later they were joined by Gerónimo de Aguilar who had been shipwrecked there many years earlier. Having been enslaved by the lord of Chetumal, Aguilar spoke Maya fluently.

The ships next sailed west along the coast from Isla de Mujeres to Cape Catoche being careful to resupply at each opportunity. Eventually the missing ship rejoined them in the bay of Campeche not far from where Grijalva had suffered defeat at the hands of the Maya. Cortés considered launching a punitive expedition, but decided to move on to Tabasco where the army disembarked and moved inland to Potonchan, a Maya trading center. They besieged a squadron which shortly withdrew to join allies who were massing at Centla a few miles away. Although many of the Spaniards were wounded in the battle that followed, none had been killed, while more than 800 of the Maya had died before their commanders gave the signal to withdraw. Returning to Potonchan, Cortés accepted tribute from the lord of the kingdom. He then set about interviewing the prisoners concerning sources of gold and soon learned that they lay much farther inland to the west. He discovered that the land was ruled by an Aztec emperor of Tenochtitlan. Aguilar confessed that he could not speak the Aztec language, but a woman named Malintzin who had been given to Cortés spoke both Aztec and Maya. Between 'Doña Marina,' as the Spaniards called her, and Aguilar, Cortés formed the nucleus of a diplomatic corps that was to become crucial to the next phase of his operation: raising a confederated Indian army to march against Motecuhzoma.

We know that Cortés had quilted cotton armor of Aztec style made up in Cuba for his troops. Any helmets issued were limited to simple war-hats and probably dated to as early as the first expeditions under Columbus. (Author's reconstruction)

ORGANIZATION, TRAINING AND TACTICS

After the battle of Centla, Miguel discussed tactics with the other soldiers, comparing his training in Italy with what they had learned in the Caribbean. He thought the deployment of cavalry as an independent combat unit was risky. Cortés and the other captains would have been annihilated in any European conflict without the support of the infantry and artillery. Veterans of the invasions of Cuba, Jamaica, and Puerto Rico explained that the Indians were generally terrified of horses and as they possessed no organized units of pike or matchlock, they were easily ridden down once their formations had been broken.

The Spanish army of the 16th century was unlike any other army in Europe at the time. It was forged through the *Reconquista*, the 'reconquest' of the Iberian peninsula by Ferdinand and Isabel who succeeded in overthrowing Granada in 1492, the last European Islamic state. This dramatic reversal was only achieved by arming the citizenry and forming them into militias, an act almost unthinkable in neighboring countries like France, where the elite class assured its very survival by restricting the right to bear arms and armor. After the defeat of the Moors, Ferdinand turned his attention to Aragon's claims to Naples and southern Italy then threatened by a French invasion. The French had every reason to be frightened of the new Spanish army. Spanish halberdiers thought nothing of dragging the flower of nobility from their horses, allowing gunners like Miguel to run their matchlocks up into their armor, literally blasting the helpless knights to pieces. The threat to an entire social order was very real and by 1500, the Spanish citizen-soldier had become the most efficient killer Europe had seen since the Roman legionaries.

Until the 15th century, the Spanish nobility was divided into numerous factions and tended to wage war defensively from the protection of castles. Campaigns were comparatively small in scale and usually entailed the raising of an army of heavily armored cavalry supported by archers whose principal function was to serve as a protective screen. The feudal organization of Spanish society demanded that virtually every nobleman perform as a fighting man, although little more training was required than to be able to sit astride a horse and handle a lance, sword, and shield with an elementary level of competence. Assembled only with difficulty, knights usually arrived in small parties and because of the long-standing disputes between them, rarely fought in any coordinated tactical formations. With the emphasis placed on chivalrous notions of 'courage,' skill, tactics, or strategy had little role to play either. Once the enemy's position was sighted, nothing could restrain the knight; the shield was shifted forward, the lance dropped, spurs were put to the charger, and the armor-clad juggernaut thundered forward. Once the battle was over, the obligation of service was deemed complete and the survivors returned to their estates.

During the 15th century the situation began to change. Greater wealth, improved communications, and better transportation allowed rival princes to hire professional troops who were trained in the use of deadlier weapons like the crossbow, the gun, and the cannon. Many were the sons of an emerging middle class: the city-based merchants and skilled craftspeople who emphasized education in art, science, and technology. The dominance of heavy cavalry ended as new forms of combat relied on densely packed formations of infantrymen. At first the men were organized into units of 50, each under the command of a captain, but by 1500, these units were expanded to 200 men, anticipating the formations later known as *tercios* during the mid-16th century.

Successful as the Spanish foot soldiers had been in the rugged Andalusian mountains against the Moors, they encountered a very different kind of foe on the broad plains of Italy: the Swiss mercenary. The first Spanish army arrived in Italy in 1495 eager to test their skill against the French. At the battle of Seminara they found themselves facing a squadron of 800 Swiss pikemen, or *landsknechts*. Superbly trained, brave, and brutal, they fought with 18 ft long spears in much the same way as the ancient Macedonian phalanx. The Swiss advanced rapidly in columns three deep, relying on the sheer impetus of their attack to drive their enemies off the field.

Beaten, but hardly defeated, the Spaniards were quick to adapt. At the battle of Cerignola in 1503, they coordinated equal numbers of gunners, pikemen, and swordsmen. First the Spanish gunners shot

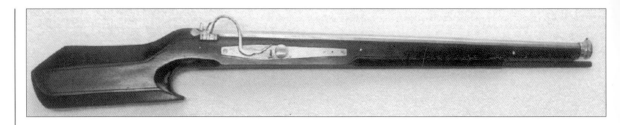

massed volleys into the enemy's phalanx while the pikemen supplied a 'hedgehog' defense. The horrifying gaps resulting from the concentrated fire were then exploited by the heavily armored swordsmen who dashed forth in dense packs to hack the *landsknechts* to death, their own pikes being useless in such close-quarter combat. The combination was unbeatable and would serve the Spaniards equally well against the echelons of Aztec troops.

The extraordinary victories that the Spanish won in Italy were only possible under the command of an equally extraordinary commander. During the Reconquista, Ferdinand and Isabel wisely understood that military skills should take precedence over noble birth in the choice of commanders. As a result they regularly elevated commoners and rewarded them with both military titles and pure gold. One man in particular, Gonzalo Fernández de Córdoba, rose above the rest to become the kind of commander the Conquistadors most desired to emulate.

Córdoba was the younger son of a prosperous Castilian landowner who stood to inherit little of his father's estate. He first sought his fortune as a soldier fighting for princes engaged in petty disputes throughout the peninsula. His remarkable skill at both mobile and siege warfare during the Granada campaign brought him to the attention of Ferdinand and Isabel. His advancement at court was rapid and in 1495 he was appointed to command the Spanish expeditionary forces in Italy. Having learned his lesson well at Seminara, Córdoba was later credited with transforming the Spanish army into the fiercesome fighting machine that emerged triumphant at Cerignola, and finally defeated the French at Garigliano in 1504, for which he was appointed viceroy of Naples.

Córdoba was known for his handsome and engaging manner, tremendous physical strength, and superb horsemanship. He displayed an elegant, luxurious personal style even on the battlefield. Being a deeply religious man who carried a small image of the Christ child on his person, he showed a natural mercy to his defeated enemies, frequently using his gentle manner to agree honorable terms rather sacking and burning their cities as the rules of war dictated. Ruthless as the Conquistadors could be, they learned the advantages of

This remarkable, fully operational facsimile of a snapping matchlock by Dale Shinn is a copy of a weapon preserved in Basle dating to 1500. The barrel is made of bronze. Shinn is a northern California-based craftsman who has become famous for his extremely accurate reconstructions of early firearms.

The internal components of a matchlock mechanism. The lock functions as follows: when pressure is applied to the button attached to the sear spring, the latter disengages the serpentine, which falls towards the pan. (Reconstruction by Dale Shinn)

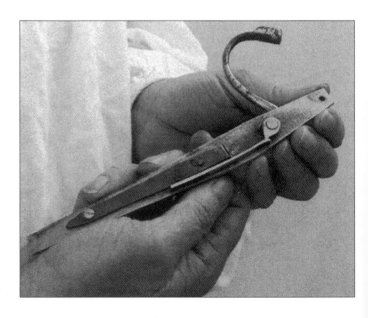

diplomacy and coalition building from the man whom they venerated as the 'Great Captain.'

If Córdoba supplied the inspiration for leadership among the Conquistadors, it was Columbus who inspired the greatest technological innovation. Until the end of the 15th century, heavy ships known as carracks were employed for short-range commerce in European waters. Little was known about open-sea navigation and the craft tended to sail along coastlines to avoid sudden storms, enemies, and other hazards. Early carracks were square-rigged which gave them speed, but only under limited conditions in favorable winds. It was the adoption of the smaller Moorish-inspired caravel that allowed Columbus' men not only to sail swiftly across open sea, but to negotiate the narrow straits and shallow inland harbors that characterized the Caribbean islands and the

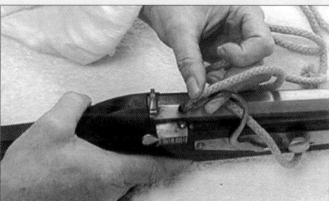

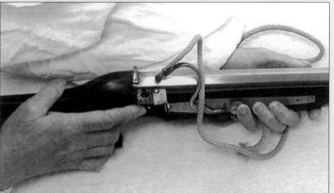

Firing a matchlock: first the gunner blows on the lit match cord to make the coal burn hotter. Next, the match cord is secured in the jaw of the cocked serpentine. The priming pan is opened to expose the fine gunpowder that leads through the touch hole to the barrel and the main charge. The gun is carefully aimed. The gunner squeezes the button trigger with the fingers of his left hand, causing the serpentine to drop the hot match cord into the priming pan. In a flash of fire and smoke the priming powder is ignited along with the main charge, and the ball is propelled out of the barrel towards the target.

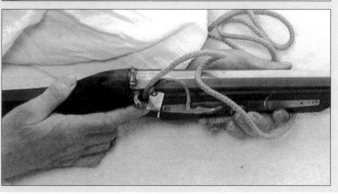

Gulf of Mexico. Innovative combinations of both square and latine rigging enabled crews to actually sail into the wind, vastly improving their crafts' maneuverability, speed, and range. As legendary as the caravel became in the history of European exploration, it was even more effective as a military innovation. Such ships allowed the Spaniards to attack foreign territory on their own terms by comprising a moveable base of operations. As it was impossible for indigenous nations to determine where or when the Spaniards might land, they could not deploy their troops in any concentrated units to resist invasion. These ships could carry sufficient supplies to keep an entire army in the field for months or, with ready access to friendly ports, even years at a time.

DRESS AND ARMOR

Despite the fact that the Spaniards composed a national military force, there was no official uniform on the cusp of the 15th and 16th centuries. Soldiers like Miguel were largely responsible for dressing themselves. Many would begin their careers wearing pull-over tunics, leggings, simple cloaks, and whatever else they could muster as farmers and laborers who had been formed into militia units. Later, wealth from plunder and exposure to the newly prosperous middle classes of merchants and tradesmen in cities throughout Italy, France, and the

Holy Roman Empire fostered personal expression in general and a taste for fashion in particular. Like the fighting men of other nations, the Spaniards at first favored the soft fluid and elegant lines reflecting the idealization of the human form so important in Renaissance art, but this soon gave way to a conservative, even rigid appearance that contrasted drastically with the ruthless troops they so often opposed. The Swiss *landsknechts*, for example, were all colors, slashes, and puffs, with jaunty hats loaded with feathers.

Most clothing was made of wool, flax, or linen. Silk and fur were expensive and largely restricted to ornamental trim only affordable by officers. Shirts were cut full and gathered at first to a low neckline, but later into a small collar or frill, from which the ruff (so popular by the end of the 16th century) developed. Tight-fitting hose was worn over the legs. The stockings were either pulled on separately, or sewn together and secured with ties to a cord, the shirt, or even the doublet.

The most common outer garments were the doublet and the jerkin. At times they were tailored along such similar lines that it is difficult to distinguish them in period artwork. Originally, the doublet fitted close to the waist and was cut low and wide at the front to reveal the shirt. Its sleeves were slim to the wrist, but rose to become much fuller, even billowing at the shoulder, where they were either sewn or tied by points to the scye. By the beginning of the 16th century, the doublet was buttoned down the front from a high collar and had a skirt which varied from very short to hip length. Sometimes the seams were concealed with the addition of padded rolls or wings. Sleeveless waistcoats, virtually identical in cut, were often worn underneath for additional warmth or as casual dress by men who could afford them. The early jerkin was also fitted to the waist but could be either high- or low-necked. It featured a pleated skirt reaching to just above the knee, but later it was shortened to above the hip. At first it was worn open to reveal the shirt, doublet,

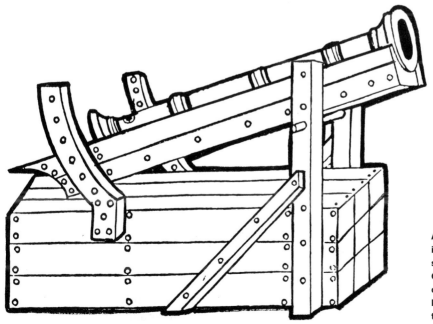

A wood block print illustrates an ingenious makeshift timber structure by which the Conquistadors could have deployed their falconets in land-based operations against the Aztecs. (Author's illustration)

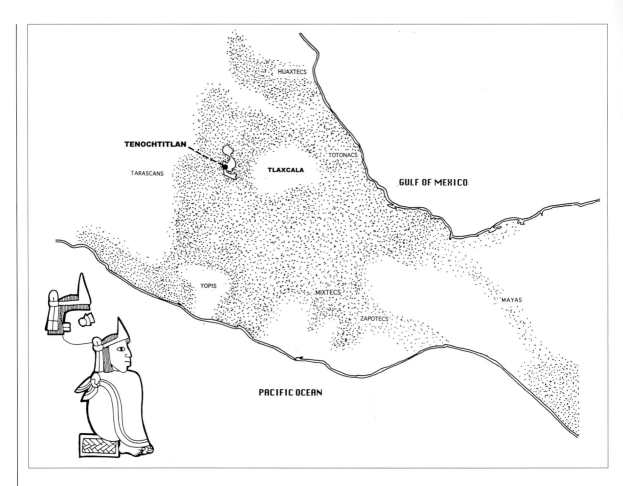

HUAXTECS

TENOCHTITLAN

TOTONACS

TARASCANS

TLAXCALA

GULF OF MEXICO

YOPIS

MIXTECS

MAYAS

ZAPOTECS

PACIFIC OCEAN

Under a succession of nine emperors called *huey tlatoque* or great speakers, the Aztec empire had expanded over much of the central and southern highlands of Mexico. After 1500, campaigns continued to be waged against the Mixtecs of coastal Oaxaca and their former allies, the Tlaxcalteca, who had become entirely surrounded. (Author's illustration)

and cod-piece but by the mid-16th century it was worn with a high-standing collar and could be buttoned from neck to waist. The skirts were no longer pleated, but still flared in varying lengths. Ultimately, the jerkin survived into the 17th century as the heavy cavalryman's buff coat, while the doublet became the basis for today's jacket.

Gowns were fashionable as overcoats. Initially worn long, they were subsequently shortened to the knee, very full with pleats at the back extending from a yoke. They were left open at the front and thrown back to reveal an ornamental lining which spread over the shoulders to a squared off shape at the back.

Sometime after 1530, hose became separated into upper and lower stocks, the former becoming breeches, the latter stockings. With the shortening of the doublet, the breeches were revealed and took on a variety of lengths and shapes. They were basically constructed in three layers, a fitted base over which any padding was arranged, an inner lining cut full, and an outer section less full, but slashed into long strips called panes that allowed the inner lining to show through.

The most popular head covering was the flat cap with its beret-shaped crown and narrow brim, worn either straight or turned up. Many were cut into sections and stiffened. Skull caps with small upturned brims were popular among sailors and soldiers alike.

Despite their appreciation for current European fashion, in reality Spanish soldiers had little recourse but to adopt the clothing of the nations in which they were campaigning. We know that they frequently received gifts of clothing from the Aztecs. The styles matching their own sensibilities would have included the *xicolli*, a short fringed jacket favored by priests, and a broad rectangular weaving called a *tilmatli* worn as a cape or poncho. Shoes and ankle boots would have been replaced with sandals.

The degree to which armor was employed by the Conquistadors is debatable. Very few of the participants who wrote of their combat experience discuss what type of protection they possessed or how much of it they actually wore. Either the Conquistadors used very little armor or its employment was so commonplace as to be hardly worth mentioning. As effective as it had been for shock troops in Spain and Italy, armor's usefulness in the Caribbean was limited. It was insufferable to wear in the wet, insect-infested, tropical environment. Heavy, it radiated heat in excess of 200 degrees in direct sunlight and had to be constantly cleaned or painted to protect it from rusting. Furthermore, it was expensive no matter how out-of-date it was, and campaign leaders working with the restrictive budgets imposed by their backers always opted for offensive weaponry over defensive protection.

Pictorial records of the opening phases of the Mexican campaign tend to suggest that Cortés' men wore very little armor. An Indian painting dating to within ten years of the event, the *Tlaxcala Manuscript,* depicts the Spaniards carrying swords, pikes, and lances, but wearing no armor upon their approach to Tlaxcala. Similarly, Bernal Díaz speaks of a soldier wearing a 'half gilt, but somewhat rusty helmet' as being a sight so unusual that it drew the attention of an Aztec ambassador. At a later date, however, Díaz refers to the Spanish horsemen in particular as being 'well protected by armor,' and the Aztecs themselves speak of men 'completely encased in iron, as if turned to iron.' The differences in the accounts suggest two possibilities; the armor was not ordinarily part of the personal equipment of the soldiers but rather, was packed with the supplies and distributed prior to a pitched battle, or else armor was simply acquired later in the campaign through resupply. The truth would probably incorporate something of both of these interpretations.

Any armor available to the first expeditions under Columbus would have been limited to war hats and breast plates. Actual artifacts excavated in the southwestern United States indicate that there had been little change over a half-century later. The war hat or *chapel de fer* was an open helmet with a low crown and a broad round brim worn from the 12th to the 16th century. It was easily manufactured, transported, and distributed, yet despite its simplicity it was a dignified and practical defense in serious fighting by noble

The connection that Indian people made between the Spaniards and the legend of the man-god Quetzalcoatl was reinforced by religious symbolism. Santiago, the patron saint of Spain, was identified by his broad-brimmed hat, pilgrim's staff, and sea-shells shown here on a statue from his shrine at Compostela. Coincidentally, the same symbols were attributed to Quetzalcoatl in his guise as the wind god, Ehecatl. (Author's illustration)

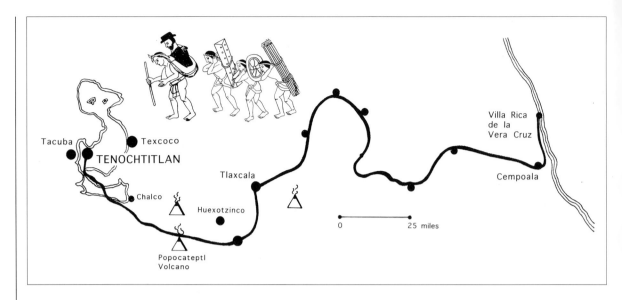

By mid-June 1519, Cortés was marching inland with an army of 300 Spaniards and 250 Totonac warriors and porters. After a series of initial conflicts, the Tlaxcalteca welcomed the Spaniards as allies in September. The confederated army then continued through Cholula and the Basin of Mexico in October and entered Tenochtitlan on November 8. (Author's illustration)

and commoner alike. During the 15th century another type of helmet evolved from the war hat, the *celata* or *salade*. At first, some versions of the war hat featured eye-slits in the brim allowing the soldier to pull the helmet down low over the forehead during combat without entirely impeding his forward vision. This simple modification was so effective that armorers began to lower the brim of the war hat entirely to enclose the lower part of the head. By 1450, both Spanish and Italian troops, however, began to favor a variation of the *celata* called a *barbute* that exposed the face.

The 16th century witnessed other modifications in the war hat, particularly the elevation of the crown and the narrowing of the brim. Such helmets first began to appear on Italian battlefields where they were called *cabassets* or '*pears*.' Presumably the *cabasset* was introduced to Spain by returning veterans who would then have taken them to the Caribbean after 1500. It would actually be 30 to 40 years later before the fourth, most famous variation of the war hat began to appear. Called a *morion*, this distinctive crested helmet sported a graceful brim that swooped low over the ears and then rose to high peaks over the face and back of the head. Although it was never actually employed by the Conquistadors themselves, it eventually became so popular among Spanish troops serving throughout the empire, that its appearance was mythically transposed on to the notorious adventurers in later years.

Knights in full suits of armor had always been the most heavily armed of any military force in medieval Europe. During a charge they were frequently subjected to murderous barrages of missile fire before they could reach the enemy. Consequently, closed helmets would have been essential to their tactics, but to what extent the Conquistadors used them is unknown. The *armet* was the most common late 15th century horseman's helmet. It conformed to the shape of the head, but the weight was distributed over the shoulders by attachment to a broad gorget at the neck. Early examples had hinged cheek pieces that were joined at the chin under the visor. Later, a single moveable chin piece rotated into place on the same pivots as the visor itself. The drawback was that such equipment required a tremendous degree of workmanship by artisan-armorers which was expensive. Totally enclosing the head, they were too hot to wear in the tropics and the systems of pivots and hinges would have been susceptible to rust, ultimately rendering them useless.

In the 16th century a new style of cavalry helmet began to appear called a *burgonet*. They were open helmets, with a brim projecting over the eyes and a standing comb. Nevertheless, they could be easily fitted with cheek plates, and when worn with a *buffe* or chin protector strapped around the base of the neck they supplied all the protection of the *armet* without the need for personal fitting or maintenance.

Like helmets, body armor was costly to purchase, ship, and maintain in the western hemisphere. During the Italian campaigns, it was normal for soldiers to strip armor from dead knights, but how much they sold off and how much they actually kept for personal use is difficult to evaluate. The most basic defense was chain mail which dated back to at least Roman times. It was produced by winding wire tightly around a metal rod and then cutting off rings that were riveted together. An ordinary shirt of mail could weigh anywhere between 15 lb and 30 lb depending on both the size of the rings and the garment. Some men may have been fortunate enough to acquire brigandines, protective vests made of plates of iron or steel riveted to a canvas garment and covered in velvet or other rich materials. Plate armor would have been Gothic in style and infantrymen deployed as shock troops fought in breast plates. When available, cavalry were fitted out in three-quarter suits of plate armor that would ideally consist of breast and back plate, rerebraces, vambraces, taces, tassets, and cuisses.

Quitlauhtique

The *Lienzo de Tlaxcala* was painted by Indian artists to commemorate their role in the conquest of the Aztec Empire. Here Cortés and Marina meet with the *tlatoque* of Tlaxcala led by Maxixcatzin and Xicotencatl. Gift exchanges of gold and jewelry were the means of negotiating systems of mutual obligation in Mesoamerican Indian societies. The Tlaxcaltec lords also hoped to arrange marriages with their daughters, a means by which alliances were consolidated. At first the Spanish officers accepted the women, but when Cortés began to comprehend the nature of the relationship that their actions implied, he returned them to their parents.

In considering the quantity and quality of armor employed during the various Conquistador campaigns, one must take into account the practicality of the various forms of indigenous armor as well. For the most part, Indian weaponry tended to be limited to slings, bows, spear throwers, clubs, and swords edged with volcanic glass razors. The Aztec *ichcahuipilli* was the most basic form of defense against such an arsenal. Vests constructed of quilted cotton, they were designed to absorb the impact of a projectile rather than stop it and therefore functioned much like a European aketon. Finally, shields were essential for swordsmen and cavalry. The Spaniards tended to favor the round, convex, target made of iron or wood and secured to the arm and hand by rings. A leather, heart-shaped shield called an *adarga* was also very popular. It had originally been adopted from the Moors and would have been easy to fabricate in the Americas.

OFFENSIVE WEAPONRY

The primary weapons of the Conquistadors included swords, lances, crossbows, matchlocks, and light artillery. Swords changed very little throughout the Middle Ages. They had a blade about 3 ft long and were carried in a leather-covered wooden scabbard that hung vertically from a belt down the left leg. Most swords were sharpened on both edges, but usually blunted at the tip in order to slash at an opponent without it becoming entangled in surcoats and chain mail. Their hilts were relatively simple, featuring a sculpted pommel and a cross guard. By the 16th century new techniques for tempering metal, many adopted from the Moors, enabled Toledo craftsmen to forge swords called rapiers that were narrower, lighter, and sharper but sacrificed little in terms of strength and resiliency. Their needle-like tips were now intended to exploit gaps in armor and could even pierce chain mail. The hilt was enhanced by the addition of metal rings, many in fanciful combinations that not only added a sense of artistry to the weapon but in the hands of a skilled swordsman could be used to entangle the blade of an opponent and even disarm him. The longer rapier was suspended from a baldric, a wide belt hung over the right shoulder with its two ends attached to the scabbard in such a way that the sword hung diagonally across the lower back with the hilt over the left hip. The broadsword itself was never entirely abandoned and doubtless many Conquistadors continued to employ them, including a hefty 5½ ft version that was wielded with both hands. Originally designed to break the pikes of their *landsknecht* opponents, broadswords could also inflict devastating casualties on densely packed masses of lightly armed Indian troops. A variety of bills and halberds were available to the Conquistadors, as well as 12 ft lances that were invaluable to cavalry squadrons who could disrupt even the largest formations of Indian armies with a series of coordinated, direct onslaughts as long as the terrain was flat and open. Doubling as pikes, lances could also be used by infantry to support units of swordsmen, crossbowmen and gunners alike.

The crossbow dated from at least the third century AD, but they were not very powerful and tended to be employed for hunting in earlier times. Eventually, medieval craftsmen learned to make the weapon's 2 ft

long arms stiffer by laminating various kinds of hardwoods, cane, horn, and bone together, but this made the weapon more difficult to cock. The solution was the use of a stirrup through which the foot was passed to secure the stock to the ground, while the string was drawn back with a crank attached to a cord and pulley system. By the 14th century the crossbow had become the essential weapon for all European armies. A 12 in. bolt could actually pierce steel armor at close range. Furthermore, they were relatively easy to manufacture and needed less care than the matchlocks with which they were so often paired during the 15th century, a distinct advantage in the humid tropics of the Caribbean, Mexico, and Central America.

Miguel credited the invention of his gun to an alchemist-monk named Black Berthold. According to a legend he learned from the old gunners, Berthold had been attempting to kill the spirit force that dwelled within mercury as the first step to making gold. First he heated the metal in a crucible, then he added charcoal, saltpeter, and finally sulfur. Needless to say, the exploding crucible nearly killed Berthold, but it also gave him the idea of using gunpowder to shoot projectiles. Whatever their true origin, guns were widely deployed on battlefields throughout Europe during the late Middle Ages. Little more than simple tubes of brass, bronze, or iron bound to straight staffs of wood, they rapidly gained popularity as they were fairly simple to make and required very little training to fire. By 1450, the prospect of an

ABOVE LEFT **The *Lienzo de Tlaxcala* portrays the baptism of the Tlaxcaltec lords. Cortés spoke ceaselessly about Christianity and even convinced the Tlaxcalteca to remove the idols from one of their temples and replace them with images of the cross and the Virgin. For the Spaniards, the baptism became a very public, demonstration of reciprocity in their alliance with Tlaxcala.**

ABOVE RIGHT **The Cholulteca fight for their lives on the steps of the temple of Quetzalcoatl. At first the Spaniards were welcomed into the city but after two days, the Totonac informed Cortés that the Cholulteca loyal to Motecuhzoma were planning a trap. Cortés assembled the noblemen in the main plaza before the temple of Quetzalcoatl and then massacred them. (*Lienzo de Tlaxcala*)**

This map of Tenochtitlan was drawn under Cortés' supervision and appeared in a published edition of his letters to the Emperor Charles. Despite the European conventions in the rendering it is surprisingly accurate, detailing the main ceremonial precinct, the principal temples and the main causeways.

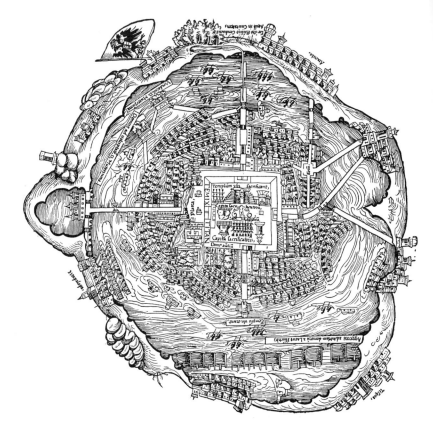

encounter with a peasant armed with a gun was a frightening proposition to a nobleman dressed in a full suit of armor. Being awkward to both aim and fire simultaneously, guns were notoriously inaccurate at first, but this situation was changed rapidly with the appearance of the matchlock by 1490.

Soldiers knew from experience with the crossbow that they could sight a gun and absorb its recoil better if they pressed the stock against the right shoulder to fire. It was just a question of devising a mechanism for automatically inserting the match into the firing hole. The first matchlocks featured an S-shaped, pivot-mounted arm called a serpentine that gripped the match between its jaws. The gun was fired by pushing the lower part of the arm forward causing the upper part to rotate backward thrusting the match into a priming chamber which in turn ignited the powder in the barrel. The development of trigger mechanisms later made the operation even simpler. At first a variety of different forms evolved including an ingenious button trigger. During the 16th century a lever very similar to that on modern fire arms was developed which acted upon the serpentine through a spring-mounted sear (from the French, *serrer*, to grip). Eventually such triggers were made smaller and were enclosed within a guard for greater safety from accidental discharge, while the serpentine was made to fall forward to allow the gunner to use his right hand for firing as well as to supply greater protection from the flash in the primer pan.

Until the standardization of Spain's arms industry under Charles V, guns were known by a variety of terms: *espingarda*, *arcabuz*, and *escopeta* were the most common. It was Córdoba who recognized the advantages of deploying large numbers of gunners as a force of fire on their own. Faced with the challenge of breaking the nearly impregnable squares of heavily armed Swiss pikemen that dominated Italian battlefields, a massed squadron of Spanish gunners could blast a hole in the formation from a safe distance of 150 yards, allowing the reserve of sword and buckler men to dash into the confused mass to finish the slaughter.

The first account of any major weaponry destined for the Caribbean is a 1495 request by Columbus for 200 breastplates, 100 matchlocks, and 100 crossbows. Obviously the armament for a squadron of 200 infantry, the order shows that the gun and the crossbow were used in equal measure in New World campaigns. Indigenous peoples possessed no cavalry, so pikes were less important. Rather Indian armies tended to fight in large dense formations of light infantry and the primary danger for the Conquistadors was being surprised and overrun before they could bring their superior combinations of weaponry to bear on an opponent. Accounts written by Conquistadors such as Cortés, Díaz, Alvarado and others describe the challenges of keeping a massed enemy at a distance. Guns could inflict horrifying damage on vastly superior numbers, but they took a great deal of time to prepare, load and fire. Able to manipulate their weapons more rapidly, crossbowmen were ideal for providing cover for the gunners. Swordsmen could then deal with the enemy that broke through their ranks on an individual basis. Once an initial onslaught was stopped, artillery could be positioned to allow the Spaniards to keep an enemy at bay almost indefinitely.

The standard ordnance on most campaigns was a breech-loading cannon with a 2–3 in. bore called the falconet. Usually mounted on the topside rails of ships to repel boarders, they were transported inland by the early Conquistadors who remounted them on makeshift carriages or even timber scaffolds. With ranges in excess of 2,000 yards, they packed a terrific force capable of killing five or more men at a time. The sound they produced seldom failed to terrify indigenous peoples who associated such weapons with the supernatural forces of thunder, lightning, and volcanic eruptions. During the conquest of Mexico heavier cannon were also employed. Known by such imaginative names as *pasabolante*, *culebrina*, and *lombarda*, scholars still debate their sizes and calibers. Cortés was known to have had four falconets and ten brass lombards when he landed in Veracruz in 1519. The falconets were subsequently lost during '*La Noche Triste*'. It seems that the lombards were deemed too heavy to maneuver very effectively and were probably deployed for the defense of his coastal fortress at Villa Rica until a proper system of transport could be arranged, after which they were applied with devastating effect against the city of Tenochtitlan in 1521.

Pánfilo de Narváez is put in chains. Cortés was continually negotiating his position between both Indian and Spanish factions. Eventually, Velásquez assigned Narváez to sail to Mexico and arrest Cortés. When Cortés learned of the new Spanish expedition, he left Alvarado in charge at Tenochtitlan, and captured Narváez in a surprise attack on May 28, 1520. (*Lienzo de Tlaxcala*)

DIPLOMACY AND CAMPAIGNING

Two months after they had left Cuba, Cortés' expedition sailed up the coast of Veracruz to San Juan de Ulua. Here they saw more gold than they had in Maya country, confirming the reports of the Grijalva's expedition. They were also met by an Aztec ambassador whose mission was to find out as much as he could about the formidable strangers and to report back to Motecuhzoma personally. The ambassador bore gifts for Cortés and even paid tribute by presenting him with the ritual dress of a god named Quetzalcoatl. When Cortés announced his intention to march on Tenochtitlan to meet with his 'friend' Motecuhzoma, the ambassador tried to dissuade him and then withdrew.

Velásquez's representatives were outraged, for this was the first they had heard of the audacious plan. They demanded that the expedition return to Cuba immediately. Cortés countered by employing a clever political maneuver. He officially founded a town that he called Villa Rica de la Veracruz and established a legal structure that placed it under direct authority of the Holy Roman Emperor Charles V. A town council composed of Cortés' most loyal adjutants then decided that the expedition had fulfilled Velásquez's mandate as outlined in his contract and declared themselves an independent company. It was then that the Spaniards were invited by a Totonac delegation to meet with their own lord at Cempoala. Learning of their military prowess and believing Cortés to be Quetzalcoatl's representative if not actually the god himself, the Totonacs explained that they had been conquered by the Aztec empire of the Triple Alliance many years before and now suffered oppressive tribute demands. It was the first indication of dissent among Motecuhzoma's vassals and Cortés foresaw considerable advantages in allying himself with the Indians who were traditional enemies of the Aztecs.

Miguel knew that Cortés was a devout Catholic who read the *requerimiento* to the enemy (formal decree to accept the Christian faith and Spanish sovereignty) so why would he allow himself to be honored as a pagan god? The Totonacs explained that Quetzalcoatl had founded the Toltec capital of Tula located about 40 miles north of Mexico City some 500 years earlier. Here the Toltecs prospered until a rift developed between two opposing factions. When Quetzalcoatl's rivals, Tezcatlipoca and Huitzilopochtli, patron gods of the Aztecs, incited the hero to drunkenness and incest, he was shamed before his followers and left the city to spend the remainder of his life wandering from kingdom to kingdom. By most accounts he established a new cult center

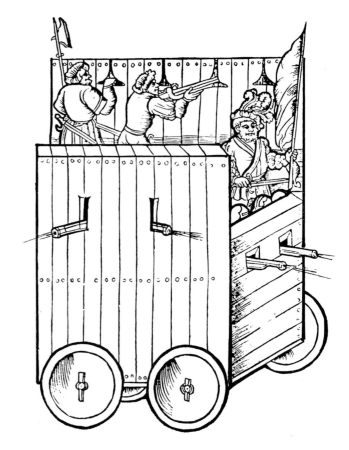

Besieged in the palace of the former emperor Axayacatl, the Spaniards attempted to drive off the Aztecs with sorties. At one point they experimented with battle wagons constructed of timber, perhaps resembling this one portrayed in a European woodcut. (Author's illustration)

at Cholula. Others report that he also traveled through Oaxaca where he even constructed the Zapotec palaces at Mitla. According to the Totonacs, Quetzalcoatl eventually reached their own capital of Cempoala and subsequently either died and was resurrected as the morning star, or boarded a raft of serpents bound for the east, promising to return one day to reclaim his kingdom.

By analyzing the sagas of Mesoamerican cultural heroes like Quetzalcoatl, historians have discovered that their cults played a significant ideological role when independent kingdoms wanted to unite into larger states in Postclassic Mexico. The aim of sharing heroic history was to elevate the ideology of one elite group above the petty disputes of individuals that prevented unity and the mutual benefits of coalition. Since heroes were sanctified by religious ritual, they could be used to incite patriotic sentiments. As a consequence, the spiritual connection to gods, heroes, and ancestors maintained through their cults could be comparable to the claims of nationality and language which contemporary societies use to define a state.

The Totonacs, together with the Eastern Nahua, the Mixtecs, and the Zapotecs, believed themselves to be the 'children of Quetzalcoatl.' It is not recorded what Cortés thought of being venerated as their god, but having studied classical history at the University of Salamanca he may have had some elementary knowledge of the relationship of hero cults to the alliances of Greek city-states. More recently, even the princes of Aragon had invoked the legend of Odysseus in their claims to the kingdom of Naples.

The Totonacs advised that the Spaniards could find sympathetic allies among the Tlaxcalteca to the west and provided them with 50 warriors and 200 porters to help move supplies and falconets 100 miles inland. According to their own histories, the Tlaxcalteca were among the first Chichimec bands to invade the Basin of Mexico under the leadership of Quetzalcoatl's father Mixcoatl. After the fall of Tula around the middle of the 12th century, they moved to the east to settle in the modern state of Tlaxcala, confederating themselves with Huexotzinco, Cholula, and a score of smaller kingdoms from Puebla to Oaxaca. Tlaxcaltec territory was divided into four pie-shaped quarters converging on a central point where government was dominated by the four highest ranking kingdoms, Tepeticpac, Quiahuiztlan, Ocotelolco, and Tizatlan. Located within a few miles of each other, the rulers of these kingdoms, called *tlatoque*, formed a governing council. The

After the death of Motecuhzoma, the Spaniards realized that their position in Tenochtitlan was no longer tenable and on the night of June 30, they attempted to escape. Using a moveable bridge they managed to cross over a canal that divided the Tlacopan causeway. The *Florentine Codex* illustrates an Aztec legend that the army was spotted by a woman drawing water, and she warned the watch at the Temple of Huitzilopochtli. (Author's illustration)

council was led by the *tlatoani* of Tizatlan at the time of the Conquest, but there is evidence of a rotational power structure rooted in a fairly equal distribution of political, religious, and economic functions.

Despite the outward appearance of a stable centralized administration, the *tlatoque* governed Tlaxcala in the midst of profound factional tension. The lesser lords, called *tetecuhtin*, frequently competed with each other over inheritance rights, ownership of lands, and access to strategic resources. The council of the *tlatoque* and the *tetecuhtin* consequently fell into dispute over what to do about the Spaniards, some favoring an alliance but a majority, it seems, demanding war. Soon after entering Tlaxcala territory, the Spanish expedition was attacked. Two major battles were fought and the Spaniards were very nearly annihilated when suddenly the Tlaxcalteca reversed themselves and proposed a truce. The Tlaxcaltec lords realized that a long-term alliance with the Spaniards against their common enemy, the Aztecs, would be of more benefit than the satisfaction of a minor victory over a small group of strangers. Cortés was soon to learn that the Tlaxcalteca were not unique in their behavior. Countless times throughout the campaign, Spanish successes would be due as much to such sudden reversals of policy among Indian factions as any other single factor.

The Tlaxcalteca had been engaged in nearly 60 years of continuous warfare with the Aztecs and described the administration of their hated empire in considerable detail for the Spaniards. The region was divided among nine major ethnic groups dominated by an alliance of three kingdoms, Tenochtitlan, Texcoco, and Tlacopan. By 1460, Tenochtitlan had emerged to become the dominant partner. Founded in 1325, the city had been ruled by a succession of nine emperors of whom the last was Moteuchzoma Xocoyotzin or Moteuchzoma II. The second-in-command was a powerful priest called the *Cihuacoatl* or 'Snake Woman' and the government was administered through various councils of ranking lords. Motecuhzoma had also engaged in numerous marriages

During *La Noche Triste*, the Spaniards and their Indian allies found themselves entrapped on the Tlacopan causeway. Using canoes, the Aztecs attacked from all sides and scores of men were driven into the canals where they drowned. (*Lienzo de Tlaxcala*)

Chief Caonabo massacres Columbus' men at La Natividad, 1493

A

Cortés is venerated as the god Quetzalcoatl

C

The March on Tenochtitlan

D

Weapons

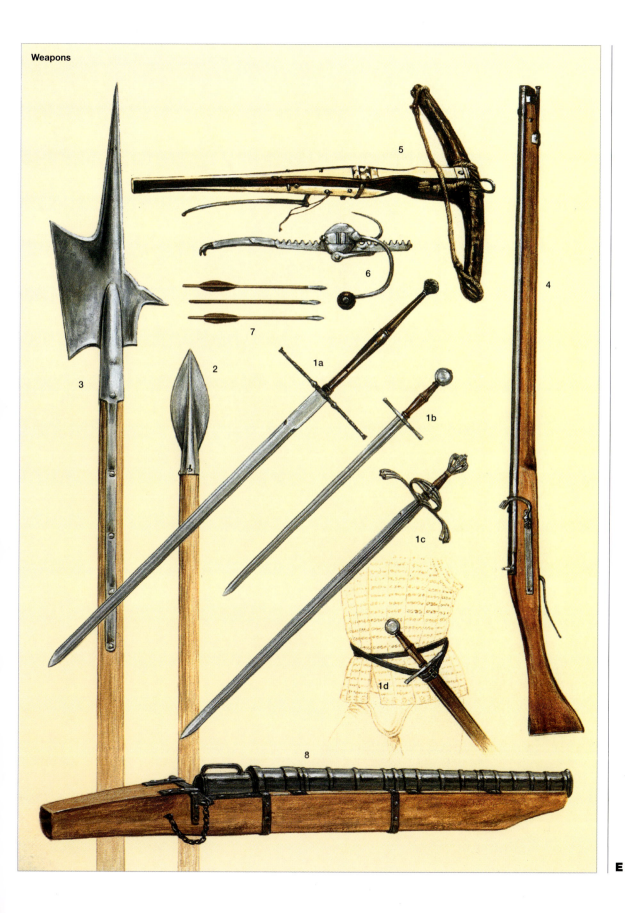

3

2

1a

1b

1c

1d

4

5

6

7

8

E

F

Armor

4

2b

2d

2a

2c

1b

3

1a

1a

3

5a

1b

4

5b

1c

2

5c

Last stand at the Great Temple, 1521

H

The battle of Cajamarca, 1532

The *encomendero*, the *cacique*, and the Vicar of Yanhuitlan

in an effort to consolidate his authority by producing scores of children. Each of his wives represented families who were continually embroiled in factional disputes of their own and doubtless had ambitions to rule as well.

On October 10, 1519, a confederate army of less than 300 Spaniards and some 6,000 Tlaxcalteca marched south 25 miles to Cholula. Here the Spaniards were greeted only with reluctance. Cortés responded by accusing a faction of the Cholulteca loyal to Motecuhzoma of planning a trap. He then directed his men to brutally massacre 3,000 men in the main square before the temple of Quetzalcoatl, and placed the leader of an opposition movement allied with Tlaxcala on the throne.

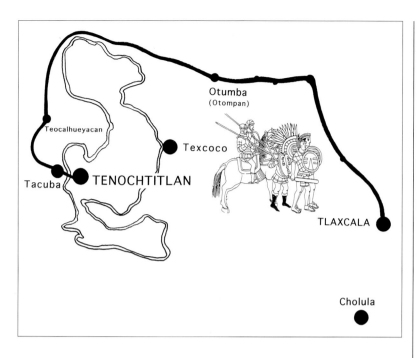

Motecuhzoma was stunned. Why he did not crush the Spaniards with the overwhelming military force he was known to have at his command has always been a source of debate. One theory is that, after Cortes' success in defeating Motecuhzoma's allies and appointing a new king to the throne of Cholula, any further opposition on Motecuhzoma's part might encourage dissident factions within his own domain, particularly around Chalco, a kingdom once allied with Tlaxcala, that had never been absorbed into the empire peacefully. Another theory is that the majority of young men who composed the Aztec imperial forces were also farmers and therefore the principal food producers for the entire city. Armies could therefore only be mobilized during the dry season from November to May when the fields lay fallow. This theory is reinforced by an account of the Yucatan Caste War of 1847. At one point the city of Merida had been surrounded and the governor was considering evacuating the city when suddenly the insurrectionists inexplicably withdrew. Years later it was discovered that the host of Maya farmer-soldiers had seen the first rain clouds of the season approaching and took it as a sign to return to their villages to plant the life-giving maize on which they would have to subsist throughout the following year, even though it meant forfeiting a hard-won victory. Whatever the actual reasons, Motecuhzoma clearly perceived a greater advantage for the moment in inviting the Spaniards into the city of Tenochtitlan. Although it temporarily placed him in a compromising position, it was a logical strategy from the perspective of the political situation at that time.

Tenochtitlan was constructed on an impregnable island near the western bank of Lake Texcoco. Access to the surrounding countryside was via three great causeways. Escorted by Motecuhzoma's nephew, Cacama, lord of Texcoco, Cortés and his men marched across the Tlalpan causeway where they met Motecuhzoma himself. Motecuhzoma

Reaching the western shore of Lake Texcoco, Cortés led the survivors of his army to safety among the Otomi allies of Teocalhueyacan. The Spaniards next attempted to march north around Lake Texcoco, but were trapped at Otumba near the ancient ruins of Teotihuacan. Barely managing to escape with their lives, they were relieved to reach Tlaxcala on July 11, 1520. (Author's illustration)

approached Cortés under a pallium of gold and green feathers carried by four lords. Cortés dismounted and moved forward to embrace Motecuhzoma in Spanish fashion but was prevented by Cacama who indicated that it was regarded as sin to touch him. Nevertheless, Cortés placed a necklace of pearls, diamonds, and gems of glass around Motecuhzoma's neck. Motecuhzoma in turn commanded that two large necklaces of gold be given to Cortés. Then a few of the 4,000 lords in attendance walked forward, touched the earth with their right hand before Cortés as a sign of honor, kissed it, and signaled the Spaniards to follow the entourage back into the city.

Tenochtitlan had a population of 100,000 people and was one of the largest cities in the world. Had the Spanish realized this, they may have reconsidered accepting the Aztecs' extraordinary hospitality, but there was no going back now. Men like Miguel had seen large cities in both Spain and Italy, but nothing could compare to the spectacle of the broad canals with the hustle and bustle of hundreds of canoes carrying every sort of cargo. The Spaniards were simply dumbfounded by the market at Tlaltelolco where 70,000 people traded in staples like maize, beans, squash, meat of all varieties, spices and seasonings, as well as luxury goods – gold and silver, finely woven and embroidered cloth, and exquisite objects of feather work. Cortés and his men were even offered a sumptuous palace as their residence, but it would soon become their prison. It was not long before news began to reach the Spaniards that the Aztecs had attacked their Totonac allies who in turn stopped providing supplies to the garrison at Veracruz. With most of the Tlaxcaltec army camped outside the city, Cortés seized Motecuhzoma. Motecuhzoma went willingly, but why he cooperated is unknown. He may have simply been concerned for his own safety, or more likely it was a calculated political decision, for even in captivity he could continue to rule as the *huey tlatoani* (great speaker).

A typical European square composed of gunners and pikemen for battlefield defense. During the battle of Otumba, the Aztecs surrounded Cortés and his men trying to induce them to panic. However, by forming up into dense squares, the Spaniards held off the Aztecs with matchlock and crossbow fire, while the horse sallied forth to disrupt enemy troop coordination. (Detail from an engraving published by Théodore DeBry, 1591)

With the emperor as hostage, the Spaniards believed that they held the upper hand. The stalemate lasted well into the following spring of 1520 during which time they managed to extort a vast hoard of gold worth more than 700,000 ducats. Then the Spaniards heard that an army of over 800 men under the command of Pánfilo de Narváez had landed on the coast with orders from Vélasquez to arrest Cortés. Cortés put Alvarado in charge of 80 men to secure their position at Tenochtitlan and marched against Narváez, capturing him by surprise attack and persuading his army of over 1,300 to join his own forces. Cortés then returned to find the Tenochtitlan garrison frightened for their lives. In his absence Alvarado had ordered the senseless execution of the Aztec nobility as they assembled unarmed for a religious celebration called Toxcatl. Any Spanish notion that they commanded the situation now vanished, as they endured 23 days of siege. In one final act of desperation, Cortés ordered Motecuhzoma to command his soldiers to lay down their arms.

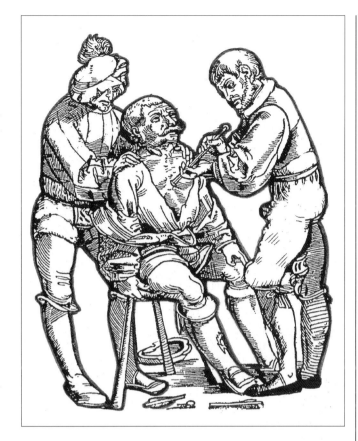

A European woodcut illustrating the painful extraction of an arrow from a chest wound. The Spaniards frequently survived such injuries, only to succumb to infection days later. (Author's illustration)

But it was too late. The emperor was killed as he addressed his people from the roof of the palace. When Motecuhzoma's younger brother, Cuitlahuac, was elected emperor, the Spaniards were left with no recourse but to attempt to fight their way out of the city.

Until then, Cortés had proved a master of diplomacy and campaign strategy, learning to play indigenous factions against one another in order to achieve his goals with a minimum commitment of his own resources. He seemed to have had a remarkable aptitude for grasping the nature of each political situation and being ready to confront his opponents with both masterful acts of benevolence on the one hand, and sheer treachery on the other. His tactics were ultimately derived from the notable successes of Spain's monarchs during the conquest of Granada, when they engineered the virtual collapse of the emirate by pitting three pretenders against one another prior to any actual commitment of military forces. King Ferdinand himself, it was said, had even been the inspiration for Machiavelli's *The Prince*.

While Motecuhzoma's seizure had been a bold maneuver, it was not without precedent in either Europe or the Spanish Main. Medieval princes were notorious for seizing royal hostages either for ransom or to effect a more favorable political situation within the captive's own domain. Conquistadors like Velásquez and Ponce de León had achieved their ends with the seizure and outrageous executions of *caciques* (local kings) by having them burned alive. In 1513 Núñez de Balboa succeeded in capturing the *cacique* Tubanama in Panama and holding him hostage until his people had paid 90 lb of gold. Emulating his success 20 years later, Pizarro seized the emperor Atahualpa and forced the Inca people to commit tons of gold and silver to secure his release. On June 30, 1520, Cortés was about to confront an entirely new situation. If the Aztec imperial army had been unable to take to the field before, it would never hesitate again.

COMBAT EXPERIENCE

It was just before midnight. Miguel peered through a hole in the barricade to watch the thick white haze slip ominously across the great plaza. It just might conceal the desperate men, but it would rain soon and the guns would be no more useful than clubs. Miguel was one of 40 soldiers assigned to carry a portable timber platform they had constructed to span the breaches in the causeway. Twenty days earlier, right after Motecuhzoma's death, the Aztecs had torn up the bridges in an effort to prevent the Spaniards from escaping. The Spaniards knew their chances were slim, but to remain here meant even more certain death. Cortés decided that the safest route out of the city was the most direct, but that meant fighting their way west on the Tlacopan causeway where they were sure to be entrapped. After that they could only pray that their allies would come to their aid. Miguel turned around and was dumbfounded to see the men from the Narváez expedition loading up their sacks with the heaviest of the gold objects from the hoard they'd extorted over the last few months. Couldn't they understand that they were about to fight for their very lives? Suddenly Cortés gave the signal and the barricades were lifted away from the great entryway. Captives, Motecuhzoma's hapless sons and daughters, were driven forward to provide a protective screen and the army moved cautiously out onto the plaza. There was no sign of a watch. The frightened men trotted into the drizzle toward the causeway.

Miguel and his men carefully lifted the platform into the first breach. Cortés rode his horse out to test its strength. Incredibly, the structure held and he immediately signaled the troops to follow. But a few hundred yards ahead, the next breach was considerably wider. Crawling down into a wretched mass of stone and adobe, Miguel began to lift a timber support into place when suddenly what sounded like a thousand trumpets thundered across the night. Canoes filled with archers pierced the curtain of rain and a hail of arrows showered down on the fugitives. The Spanish

The *Lienzo de Tlaxcala* portrays Cortés presenting the *matlaxopilli,* or net-bird claw signal banner, that he seized at the battle of Otumba to Lord Maxixcatzin. The Tlaxcalteca in turn offered the Spaniards food and shelter in preparation for a new assault on the Aztec imperial capital.

veyotlipan.

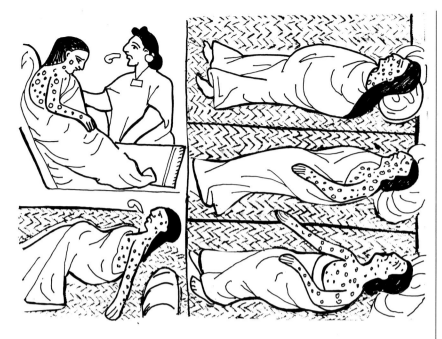

crossbowmen fired back with a heavy barrage giving Miguel and the others just enough time to secure the platform once again. Cortés spurred forward only to crash into a formation of Aztec infantry advancing from the opposite side. The captain slashed his way through, ensuring the safety of the translator Doña Marina and much of his baggage, but many of those who followed were simply driven off the viaduct into the lake. Those loaded down with heavy gold slipped below the churning water screaming for their lives in the wet silence. Suddenly the platform began to sway under the weight of men and horses crowding back upon themselves. Miguel barely dodged the splintering beam as the platform collapsed into the water. The rear echelon was cut off as an angry mob began to pour out of the city in hot pursuit. Miguel could only watch helplessly as the men fell to the horrifying blows of the razor-edged *macuahuitl* until it seemed as if Alvarado alone was still standing. The red-haired captain sheathed his sword, picked up a pike, and threw himself forward with all his might to vault across the chasm. Miguel scrambled up out of the breach and followed Alvarado through the streets of Tenochtitlan punching and kicking his way forward for what seemed like an eternity; the slaughtered bodies of those who proceeded them marked the way.

Only after hours of continuous fighting did the men find themselves outside the city where they were forced to swim for their lives to reach the western shore of Lake Texcoco. Here Cortés directed the evacuation to Teocalhueyacan an Otomi city-state who had earlier allied themselves with the Spaniards. La Noche Triste, the 'Night of Sorrow' as it would be known, ended with the Spaniards losing more than half of their men, 1,000 of their Indian allies, most of the horses, and all of the cannon.

Fearing to attempt a return to Tlaxcala by the southern route where they could be easily ambushed in the narrow passes surrounding the volcanoes, the Spaniards chose to march north along the entire length of Lake Texcoco. By the first week of July, having had only wounded horses to eat, the half-starved survivors were moving slowly across a broad arid plain near Otumba when suddenly they found themselves surrounded by a massed imperial army numbering in the thousands and led by none other than Tenochtitlan's high priest, the *Cihuacoatl* himself. The Aztecs immediately employed a strategy of double envelopment, extending a long line and then moving forward to encircle the Spaniards. The tactic allowed them to pin their enemy down with missile fire while they organized coordinated strikes with heavily armed shock troops maneuvering in such a way that the Spaniards could never tell from which direction they would be attacked next. Ultimately they hoped to force the Spaniards into a panic retreat along a prescribed route at which time they could be more easily slaughtered. The Spaniards had learned to counter by keeping the enemy at bay with matchlock and crossbow fire, while the horse sallied forth to disrupt troop coordination. Having lost so much of their equipment however, the situation at Otumba seemed hopeless until Cortés realized that the *Cihuacoatl* was coordinating his men with a system of signal banners from an adjacent hill top. The commander mustered Alvarado and four of his lieutenants. Leaving Ordás in command of the rest, the band of horseman broke through the enemy line and ran down the war leaders with their lances. The blow to the Aztec army was devastating. The loss of both their command structure and the signal system threw the Aztec troops into confusion, allowing the Spaniards to escape across the plain and back into Tlaxcala territory. Such was their hatred for the Aztec empire, the Tlaxcalteca still welcomed Cortés, even though they themselves had suffered tremendous casualties in the folly. The unlikely allies wasted little time preparing for another invasion the following year.

In the meantime a new killer had arrived in Tenochtitlan, smallpox. The disease appears to have originated in southwestern Spain. It reached Española and Cuba by 1519, where an epidemic put an end to the last Arawaks. We know that one of Narváez's men suffered from it when he arrived in Veracruz and soon passed it on to the Totonacs. Before long, town after town became depopulated. In some cases no one was even left to bury the corpses. In the Basin of Mexico alone over 40 percent of the farming population succumbed and famine soon followed. The disease also devastated royal families

In December 1520, Cortés returned to the Valley of Mexico at the head of a confederated Indian army of tens of thousands of men to begin a new assault on Tenochtitlan. Throughout the following spring, the Aztecs fought from behind barricades, from roof tops, and canoes in the narrow canals, continually trapping the Spaniards and inflicting devastating casualties. The siege became a war of attrition. (*Lienzo de Tlaxcala*)

Pushed by his impatient soldiers to seize loot, Cortés risked an attack without properly ensuring that a gap in the causeway had been filled in. Trapped yet again, (on the anniversary of *La Noche Triste*) the Spanish troops were attacked from all sides. Cortés was nearly captured by the Aztecs and barely rescued by the Tlaxcalteca. (*Lienzo de Tlaxcala*)

from Tlaxcala to Tenochtitlan, throwing the succession of a score of kingdoms into confusion. Perceiving tremendous advantage in the situation, Cortés then established himself as a kind of kingmaker making appointments to thrones in any way that could serve him. On December 4, 1520, Motecuhzoma's successor, the emperor Cuitlahuac himself died from the disease. Cortés knew the time had come to return to Tenochtitlan.

Four days after Christmas, an army of 550 Spaniards and 10,000 Tlaxcalteca entered the Valley of Mexico to prepare for what would become the longest continuous battle ever known. Perceiving that his previous entrapment was part of the strategic design of the metropolis, Cortés and his officers knew that they would first have to cut Tenochtitlan off from its allies surrounding the lake. The Spaniards first established a base of operations at the city of Texcoco by driving out the faction loyal to Tenochtitlan and placing a rival more favorable to their enterprise on the throne. Next, they attacked Ixtapalapa, a city-state built into the lake on a peninsula. But the Aztecs employed a feint, drawing the Spaniards and Tlaxcalteca into the city where, incredibly, water began to flood the streets in torrents that swept away anyone and anything caught before it. The Aztecs had smashed the dikes and flooded the city. With the gunpowder destroyed, there was no recourse but to evacuate back to Texcoco. Throughout the months of February, March, and April, operations continued against Xaltocan in the north, Yautepec, Cuauhnahuac, and Xochimilco to the south, and Tlacopan to the west, but having elected a new emperor named Cuauhtemoc, the Aztecs continued to hold the Spaniards at bay.

Cortés had known that he would have to dominate Lake Texcoco itself if he was to succeed in besieging Tenochtitlan and so he had ordered the construction of a fleet of 13 brigantines that could be hauled in sections overland from Tlaxcala. Working steadily for weeks, the Spaniards were ready to launch their fleet on April 28. Charles V's approval of the campaign led to ever more supplies and men reaching

Many Spanish captives were taken in the summer of 1521. The *Florentine Codex* indicates that they were ritually executed before the great temple of the Aztec god Huitzilopochtli. Even the heads of their horses were displayed as war trophies on the *tzompantli* or skull rack. (Author's illustration)

Veracruz from Cuba, and the Spaniards now composed a force of 86 horsemen, 700 foot soldiers, and 118 crossbowmen and gunners. There were three pieces of heavy artillery and 15 smaller field pieces. Then Cortés sent messages to all the city-states who had sworn loyalty to him calling for a general mobilization. Within days an Indian army of over 25,000 had assembled in addition to the Tlaxcalteca army. Cortés then divided the troops into three divisions, with Alvarado assigned to Tacuba, Olid allotted to Coyoacan, and Sandoval ordered to secure Ixtapalapa and then join Olid.

Cortés himself set sail on Lake Texcoco with the fleet on May 31. Having taken the precaution of attacking a fortress that threatened to alert the Aztecs of his approach, the commander suddenly spotted a force of 1,500 large canoes heading in his direction. Unfortunately the Aztecs hesitated, unsure as to how to attack the much larger vessels and giving the Spaniards time to take advantage of a prevailing wind that propelled them full speed forward into the densely packed mass of the enemy. The devastation was appalling as hundreds of canoes were overturned and the waters seemed to boil with men flailing to keep from drowning. Many of those who could get away were killed with cannon and matchlock. With the Aztec fleet defeated, Cortés' ships could now secure the causeways for the rest of the army's attack on the city itself.

For the next three weeks, the Spaniards and their Indian allies fought bloody skirmishes around the outskirts of the city. But each day that Alvarado, Olid, Sandoval or the other officers managed to secure one neighborhood they were simply driven out of it the next. The Aztecs fought from behind well-prepared positions; streets were sealed off with moveable barricades which transformed them into death traps as troops suddenly found their escape blocked and they were crushed to death by assailants showering down rocks and debris from the rooftops above. Efforts to fill in the canals by day to facilitate the maneuver of the cavalry were simply undone by the enemy at night. By the end of June, the Spaniards had secured very little ground and when the gunpowder began to run out once again, they resorted to building a catapult.

Frustrated, Cortés next planned a combined assault bringing all his forces to bear upon a single objective. But as he charged forward with his men, he neglected to fill a breach in a causeway. A hidden force in canoes closed off the breach and the Spaniards found themselves trapped between two Aztec forces. Cortés himself was badly wounded and dragged from his horse; only by luck was he rescued, for 68 of his men were captured along with eight horses. The loss was devastating.

All that night Miguel watched helplessly and listened in horror to the sounds of his comrades being executed in a religious ritual dedicated to the Aztec patron god, Huitzilopochtli. Their faces were flayed and tanned with the beards attached. Sent to the kingdoms surrounding the lake, they supplied proof of Spanish mortality and created doubt in the minds of those with whom they were allied. Troops from Tlaxcala, Texcoco, Huexotzinco, and Cholula all began to return to their homes. Unable to fight, Cortés sent messages to Cuauhtemoc to try to bluff a diplomatic end to the fighting, but his gestures were met with silence.

Cut-off from the springs of Chapultepec, the Aztecs had begun to bring fresh water back into the capital by canoes from Xochimilco. The Spaniards were soon forced to dispatch troops to quell revolts among pro-Tenochtitlan factions throughout the Basin of Mexico, as well as maintaining the daily forays into the city itself. Finally, Cortés recovered sufficiently from his wounds to restart the offensive. This time, he was determined that his men would not be trapped as they had been before. He would leave no roofs for the Aztecs to fight from, no houses for them to hide in, no gaps in the causeways, and streets to trap his men. Everything would be razed as the Spaniards moved forth block by block.

Messengers were dispatched to the allies detailing the new plan and, incredibly, they began to gather once more. Serving as a corps of engineers, masses of Indian laborers began to tear the buildings down and used the debris to fill in the canals. 'Go ahead …' the Aztecs taunted, '… rip the buildings down, you'll only have to build them back up again … if not for us then for your new Spanish masters!' But the Tlaxcalteca were undeterred, such was their hatred for an enemy who had plotted the same fate for them only a few years before. Deploying themselves in side streets, the Spaniards waited, concealed in silence. If the Aztecs attempted to attack the work crews, they quickly sallied forth to either kill or drive them off. Soon the allies could see the effects of their protracted destruction. The enemy no longer buried their dead; gnawed roots and bark chewed from trees were found in the streets, sure signs of starved men.

Cortés once again made overtures to Cuauhtemoc, but he only responded through his generals that if there was even one Aztec soldier left he would die fighting. The siege continued as before, a clash here, a skirmish there, ambush and retreat. Eventually, the Aztecs were driven into the northern part of the city where

The crossbow could be drawn by slipping the foot into a stirrup mounted at the end of the staff and either drawing back the string by hand, or with the use of a crank called a windlass. (Author's illustration)

The *Florentine Codex* illustrates the cremation of the Aztec dead. The Aztecs were very careful to do this not only as an act of reverence, but to conceal their losses. (Author's illustration)

they fortified themselves within the ceremonial precinct of Tlaltelolco. But it was not long before a broad open swath had been cleared to facilitate the Spaniards' massed formations of cavalry and infantry. Cortés planned the final assault.

Armed once again with a matchlock, equipment recently received from Veracruz, Miguel had been assigned to provide cover for a division of Tlaxcalteca and Huexotzinca forces. Their leader, Chichimecatectl, was anxious. He was the fearless man who had engineered the incredible overland transportation of the brigantines. What glory was there in starving an enemy to death? As Cuauhtemoc would not surrender, there seemed no reason to prolong the inevitable, particularly as the way to the central plaza was open and unopposed. A blast of the trumpet sent the warriors charging forward. Alvarado spurred his horse. 'Santiago and at them!' he cried, and the Spaniards dashed headlong into the flank. Breaking through the last of the barricades, Miguel came up against a fierce cuachic warrior dressed in a suit of yellow parrot feathers, his face streaked blue and yellow and emaciated from hunger. Miguel raised his gun and pushed the trigger. The fuse sputtered out. Miguel ducked instinctively. The cuachic screamed and swung his *macuahuitl*, nearly taking off Miguel's head. Miguel lifted his heavy gun by the barrel and swung it up over his head bringing the butt down hard on the Aztec's shield. The cuauchic buckled and fell to his knees. Miguel raised the gun up once more and brought it down with a crashing blow against the cuachic's head, killing him instantaneously. The Aztec warrior, obviously starved from hunger, fell forward into the dust, dead. The veteran gunner tasted the powder. There was only a hint of sulfur and it had probably been cut by unscrupulous dealers from Ponce de León's doomed expedition. Miguel rolled the corpse of the cuachic over. He ripped ten jade beads and a miniature eagle head from the Aztec warrior's neck. He was later told the jewelry signified the name of the warrior he had just killed – Ten Eagle.

Everywhere men, women, and children were being slaughtered, some driven like cattle to be drowned in a nearby canal. Rumors that women and children had hidden gold in their clothing to take out of the city unleashed a frenzy of rape and murder against the defenseless. By the end of the day more than 40,000 people lay dead in the streets and plazas. The slaughter would only stop on August 13, 1521, when Garcí Holguín, a brigantine captain, succeeded in capturing Cuauhtemoc as he fled across the lake. The emperor was brought before Cortés. 'I have assuredly done my duty in defense of my city. I am brought here before you a prisoner. I beg you to end my life. That would be just, and then you can finish with the great kingdom of Mexico,' the emperor proclaimed through the translations of Marina and Aguilar.

And so, after many long months it was over. Miguel could only stare at the devastation around him. Once he had marveled at the great white walls of the temples and palaces surrounding the market place, shimmering as if sheathed in silver. Now they were transformed into smoldering heaps of charred volcanic stone and plaster. The putrid stench was everywhere, of corpses left to rot for days in the sun. He was a battle-hardened veteran of fighting on two continents and yet never had Miguel seen killing of such magnitude before. If his fantasies were of coming to this new world to discover a lost paradise then surely he now found himself standing in an all too real hell.

'Tzilacatzin the mighty' portrayed in the *Florentine Codex*. As the battle for Tenochtitlan continued, certain soldiers on both sides began to emerge as heroic characters. The Spaniards were especially fearful of this Otomi-class warrior who was known for carrying a shield loaded with huge wall stones that he hurled at their formations. (Author's illustration)

THE FATE OF THE CONQUISTADORS

The primary objective of Cortés' expedition had been gold, but by the end of the campaign there was little to be found. Cuauhtemoc's canoe contained a small amount of treasure, but nothing compared to what the Spaniards knew they had abandoned during the 'Night of Sorrows.' The emperor and the other Aztec lords were questioned repeatedly, but offered no adequate explanation as to what had become of it all. Eventually, Cortés had Cuauhtemoc tortured and hanged. More gold was then extorted from former allies like the king of Texcoco whose aid had been instrumental to defeating Tenochtitlan. Even so the final haul was estimated to be less than 200,000 pesos. The sum paid to the crown was 37,000. Cortés took 29,600. Financiers had to be paid off in equal measure to their investment and there were many bills, but graft and kickbacks were obvious in the accounting as well. Francisco de Montejo was paid 6,000 pesos even though his direct participation had been minimal. Numerous payments ranging between 2,000 and 3,000 pesos went to lawyers, secretaries, 'bodyguards' and other 'associates.' In a subsequent lawsuit, it was reported that squadron leaders like Alvarado, Sandoval, and Olid who actually did the fighting were only paid 400 pesos, although everyone assumed that they had been secretly amassing loot throughout the war. When it was all tallied, foot soldiers like Miguel each received 60 pesos, the price of a new sword.

The *Florentine Codex* illustrates the final defeat of Tenochtitlan, which was accomplished through a series of coordinated amphibious and land-based attacks. The 13 brigantines ranged between 42 ft and 48 ft in length, and generally had only one or two sails. They were flat-bottomed which allowed them to get in close to secure the causeways. (Author's illustration)

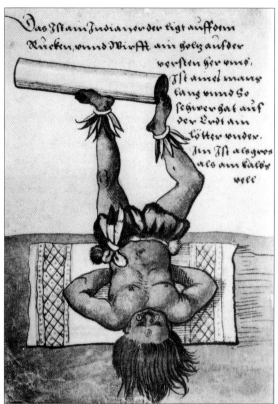

Accusations were leveled against Cortés, and the *caudillo* would spend the remainder of his life defending himself and his entitlements. To prevent the common soldiers from rising against him, he wisely directed junior officers to lead them on expeditions into the far reaches of the former Aztec empire to found new settlements. Shortly thereafter, officials began to arrive from both Cuba and Spain with contradictory papers of authority over the new lands. A governor was appointed by the Spanish court, but he was soon intimidated by Cortés' partisans and withdrew. Cortés filed a formal appeal, but Velásquez, the Bishop of Burgos, and many other enemies were determined to destroy Cortés. The wrangling for power escalated to such a level that the Holy Roman Emperor Charles V and Pope Adrian even entered into a dispute. Finally, on October 15, 1522 Cortés was named governor, captain-general, and Marquis of the Valley of Oaxaca, where, by no coincidence, many gold mines and treasure tombs had been located among the Mixtecs and Zapotecs. He virtually ruled in this capacity until 1534 during which time he commanded expeditions into northern Veracruz and western Mexico, as well as to Honduras. His supreme powers were only curtailed by the appointment of a viceroy in 1534, Antonio de Mendoza. Cortés subsequently returned to Spain where he lived out the rest of his life near Seville dying on December 22 1547.

Cortés' tactics during the war set a precedent for men of equal ambition and ruthlessness. Perhaps the most notorious was Pedro de Alvarado, the officer who had butchered the Aztec noblemen during the feast of Toxcatl. In 1522, Alvarado embarked for Oaxaca's Pacific coast with an army of 240 men. He subjugated the Mixtec capital of Tututepec

ABOVE LEFT **A portrait from life of Cortés as he appeared in 1528 at the court of Charles V. The Holy Roman Emperor granted Cortés a twelfth of the profits from his conquest and an *encomienda* of 23,000 Indian vassals, making him one of the richest men in Spain. (Weiditz, 1927)**

ABOVE RIGHT **Cortés returned to Spain with an entourage that included 40 Indians. Three of Motecuhzoma's sons made the journey, together with a group of acrobats, whose ability to twirl heavy objects with their feet truly amazed the Europeans. (Weiditz, 1927)**

and then marched south to Tehuantepec where he extorted a large amount of gold from its Zapotec lord. Two years later he defeated the Quiché Maya of highland Guatemala and had their ruler, Lord Tecum, burned alive.

In 1526, another of Cortés' officers, Francisco de Montejo, received permission to invade the Yucatan Peninsula. Friars accompanying the expedition wrote of unspeakable cruelties that were inflicted on the Maya people and yet they continued to fight for more than 20 long years. Montejo would later attribute some of his difficulties to Gonzalo Guerrero, a former Spanish soldier who had miraculously survived shipwreck and captivity to become a mighty Maya warlord.

In 1529, Nuño de Guzmán, an ally of Velásquez against Cortés, found himself in a compromising political situation and hoped to win royal favor with an attack on the kingdoms of West Mexico. Invading with an allied army of thousands of Indian and Spanish troops, he cut a bloody swath from Michoacan to Sonora. In one brutal incident he had the king of the Purépecha nearly dragged to death behind a horse before burning him

Although they had doubtless become very rich, Conquistadors like Pedro de Alvarado never ceased campaigning to the day they died. The *Lienzo de Tlaxcala* portrays Tonatiuh, as the Aztecs called him, invading Guatemala in 1523.

Quauhtemallā.

alive. Scores of villages were then put to the torch and thousands of people were enslaved.

Shortly thereafter, reports of cities of gold began to come in from the northern frontier. Indeed, the shipwrecked second-in-command of Narváez's lost expedition, Cabeza de Vaca, walked out of the desert in 1537 to confirm the existence of the Indian peoples living in large communities. Eager to capitalize on Nuño's successes, a new expedition was formulated under Francisco Vásquez de Coronado. In 1540, over 300 Spanish troops, hundreds of Indian mercenaries, and a thousand horses and swine marched into what is today Arizona and New Mexico only to find the Pueblo peoples living in cities of adobe. While the troops were away, the Indians of West Mexico rose up in open revolt and attacked isolated Spanish ranches. When the regional governor failed to subdue the insurgents, Pedro de Alvarado's aid was enlisted, but the 'Great Mixtón War', as it came to be known, was only concluded when the viceroy himself took the field with fresh troops.

Events in South America would turn out very differently for the Conquistador Francisco Pizarro. Pizarro had campaigned with Vasco Nuñez de Balboa in 1513 and later became a prominent citizen and landowner in what is today Panama. Restless in middle age, Pizarro embarked on two expeditions south along the coast of Colombia and Ecuador where he bartered for Inca gold. He won the emperor's permission to organize a third expedition to advance into Peru in 1532. Here the Inca controlled an empire of over 700,000 square miles, occupied by ten million people.

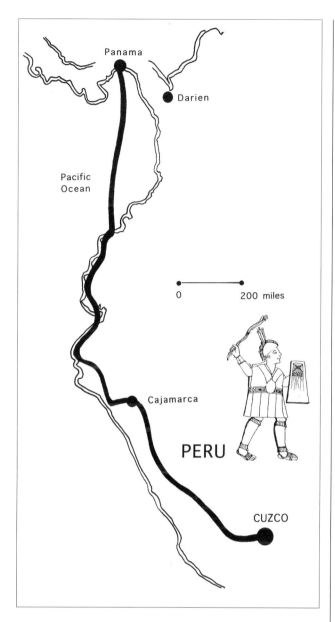

Learning that Emperor Atahualpa was camped at Cajamarca, Pizarro boldly attacked the Inca army and seized the ruler holding him hostage until he promised to fill a room with gold and other valuables for his ransom. Incredibly, the treasure yielded 13,400 lb of gold and 26,000 lb of silver. Pizarro then had Atahualpa garroted. After a series of skirmishes, the Spaniards captured the Inca capital of Cuzco itself in 1533. Resistance continued until the 1570s but the ultimate outcome was inevitable.

Enriched by his share in Atahualpa's ransom, Pizarro's cavalry commander, Hernando de Soto, personally financed an invasion of Florida in 1539 despite the dismal failure of two previous expeditions under de León and Narváez. Over the next three years, the army wandered almost aimlessly through Georgia, the Carolinas, Tennessee, Alabama, Mississippi, Louisiana, Arkansas, and Texas before fleeing for their lives down the Mississippi River with a confederated Indian army

Pizarro entered Inca territory in 1532 and found the Indian aristocracy in dispute over succession to the Inca throne after the Emperor Huayna Capac died of smallpox. With 160 men, he defeated the Inca army at Cajamarca and executed the new emperor Atahualpa. After a series of battles in 1533, the Spaniards eventually took the capital of Cuzco, but armed resistance continued elsewhere in the former empire into the 1570s. (Author's illustration)

in hot pursuit. Despite acquiring some 50 lb of freshwater pearls, the expedition was a financial disaster that cost de Soto his life.

By 1547, the year that he died, Cortés had outlived most of his contemporaries. Velásquez died penniless in 1524. Narváez was killed during his 1527 expedition to Florida. Alvarado perished during the Mixtón War when his horse fell on him in 1541. That same year Pizarro was assassinated by political enemies. De Soto died of fever in 1542 on the Mississippi River.

BIBLIOGRAPHY

Chavero, Alfredo, *Lienzo de Tlaxcala*, Mexico, 1892.

Columbus, Christopher, *Four Voyages to the New World: 1493–1503*, reprinted, Corinth, 1961.

de Fuentes, Patricia, *The Conquistadors: First-person Accounts of the Conquest of Mexico*, 1993.

Díaz del Castillo, Bernal, *The Discovery and Conquest of Mexico*, edited by Genaro García, 1956.

Durán, Diego, *The History of the Natives of New Spain*, University of Oklahoma Press, 1994.

Gush, George, *Renaissance Armies: 1480–1650*, Patrick Stephens, 1975.

Hassig, Ross, *Mexico and the Spanish Conquest*, Longman, 1994.

Heath, Ian, *Armies of the 16th Century. Volume 2: The Armies of the Aztec and Inca Empires, 1450–1608*, Foundry Books, 1999.

Held, Robert, *The Age of Firearms: A Pictorial History from the Invention of Gunpowder to the Advent of the Modern Breechloader*, The Gun Digest Company, 1970.

Lavin, James D., *A History of Spanish Firearms*, Herbert Jenkins, 1965.

Livesey, Anthony, *Great Commanders and their Battles*, Macmillan, 1987.

Lockhart, James, *The Nahuas after the Conquest: A Social and Cultural History of the Indians of Central Mexico*, Stanford University Press, 1992.

López de Gómara, Francisco, *Cortés: The Life of the Conqueror by his Secretary*, translated and edited by Lesley Byrd Simpson, 1964.

Nicolle, David, *Fornovo 1495*, Osprey Publishing, 1996.
    Pavia 1525, Osprey Publishing, 1996.
    Granada 1492, Osprey Publishing, 1998.

Oman, C. W. C., *The Art of War in the Middle Ages*, revised and edited by John H. Beeler, Cornell University Press, 1968.

Pagden, Anthony, *Hernan Cortés, Letters from Mexico*, Yale University Press, 1989.

Peterson, Harold L., *Arms and Armor in Colonial America 1526–1783*, Bramhall House, 1956.
    The Treasury of the Gun, Ridge Press and Golden Press, 1962.

Prescott, William H., *History of the Conquest of Mexico*, J.B. Lippincott Co, 1899.

Sauer, Carl Ortwin, *The Early Spanish Main*, University of California Press, 1966.

Sahagún, Bernardino de, *Florentine Codex: General History of the Things of New Spain*, trans. Arthur J. O. Anderson and Charles E. Dibble, The School for American Research and the University of Utah, 1950–1982.

Smith, Michael E., *The Aztecs*, Blackwell Publishers, 1994.

Stone, George Cameron, *A Glossary of the Construction, Decoration, and Use of Arms and Armor in all Countries and in all Times Together with Some Closely Related Topics*, Jack Brussel, 1961.

Stuart, Gene S., *The Mighty Aztecs*, The National Geographic Society, 1981.

Townsend, Richard, *The Aztecs*, Thames and Hudson, 1992.

Thomas, Hugh, *Conquest: Montezuma, Cortés, and the Fall of Old Mexico*, Simon and Schuster, 1993.

Who's Who of the Conquistadors, Cassell and Co., 2000.

Weiditz, Christoph, *Das Trachtenbuch des Christoph Weiditz von seinen Reisen nach Spanien (1529) und den Niederlanden*, edited by Theodor Hampfe, Berlin, Walter de Gruyter & Co., 1927.

Wise, Terence, *The Conquistadors*, Osprey Publishing, 1980.

An early colonial illustration by Guamán Poma de Ayala depicts the execution of Atahualpa. (Author's illustration)

GLOSSARY

Adarga a leather, heart-shaped shield
Armet the most common late-15th-century horseman's helmet
Barbute type of helmet that exposed the face
Buffe chin protector worn with a helmet
Burgonet open helmet, with a brim projecting over the eyes and a standing comb
Córdoba expedition a 1517 slaving expedition led by Fernández de Córdoba that became the first Spanish exploration of the North American mainland
Caudillo a captain
Celata a type of Spanish helmet
Chapel de fer an open helmet with a low crown and a broad round brim worn from the 12th to the 16th century.
Doublet close-fitting jacket worn by Spanish men of the 16th century
Grijalva expedition a 1518 trading expedition to Mexico led by a nephew of Cuba's governor, Juan de Grijalva
Hidalgo a rank of minor nobility
Ichcahuipilli Aztec protective vest made of quilted cotton
Jerkin a type of overcoat or vest worn in a variety of styles either with or without sleeves
Landsknechts Swiss pikemen
Matchlock the first true guns, featuring a metal grip to hold a match for igniting priming powder and a trigger mechanism called a lock
Mastiff a large 'war dog'
Morion distinctive crested, brimmed helmet
Moors Islamic peoples of Spain
Reconquista the 'reconquest' of the Iberian peninsula by Ferdinand and Isabel
Tercio 16th century Spanish army unit comprising 250 men
Tilmatli a broad rectangular weaving worn as a cape or poncho
Xicolli a short fringed jacket favored by priests

THE COLOR PLATES

A: CHIEF CAONABO MASSACRES COLUMBUS' MEN AT LA NATIVIDAD, 1493

In December 1492, Columbus' ship *Santa Maria* had run aground but thanks to the efforts of Arawak Indians under Chief Guacanagari, most of the supplies were rescued. The first European settlement in the Caribbean was established at La Natividad on the north coast of Española (Haiti-Santo Domingo). Using the timbers of the wrecked ship, the crew constructed an embankment and wooden palisade fortress with a tower and moat. Columbus then assigned 39 of the men to remain behind and search for the sources of the gold they had been collecting on the island, while he sailed back to Spain to announce his discoveries and resupply. When he returned the following year, Columbus found La Natividad destroyed, the decaying corpses of his men lying amidst the charred ruins. According to Guacangari, the Spaniards had looted the surrounding villages, seizing gold and women,

and eventually fighting over the loot among themselves. The neighboring chief, Caonabo, became so enraged by their behavior that he exacted total retribution. Columbus should not have been surprised: many of the men had been recruited from jails with promises of commuting their sentences. Most had not even been to sea before, much less served in any military capacity.

B: THE INVASION OF CUBA

By the early 16th century, much of the indigenous population of Española was dying from war, disease, and labor on the *encomiendas,* so the Conquistadors began to explore other islands in search of slaves as well as gold. After conquering the southeastern part of Española, Ponce de León learned that there was gold as well as a large population of Arawaks on the island of Puerto Rico and applied for permission to investigate. By 1509, he had subjugated the Indians, enslaved many of them, and looted enough gold to make him one of the richest men in the Caribbean. His success encouraged others to engage in similar enterprises. Two years later, Diego Velásquez de Cuéllar overran Cuba, carrying out numerous unprovoked massacres of the Indian population just as he had on Española. It was here that Cortés was to gain his most valuable military experience. Dogs played a critical part in these campaigns as they were adept at breaking up ambushes in dense forests giving the Spaniards time to reposition themselves for defense. Usually wolf hounds, dogs had first been employed as early as 1493 and proved so effective that some regarded them as being equal to ten men against Arawak warriors armed only with spears. Among the most famous was *Becerrillo* or 'Little Calf' who reputedly killed so many that he earned for Ponce de León an additional crossbowman's pay and one and a half shares of booty. Other Conquistadors, including Cortés, later executed their prisoners by turning the 'dogs of war' on them.

C: CORTÉS IS VENERATED AS THE GOD QUETZALCOATL

When Cortés arrived off the coast of Veracruz, he received an Aztec ambassador who was directed by Motecuhzoma to honor him as Quetzalcoatl, the Plumed Serpent. The year 1519, it seems, was the equivalent to the Aztec year 1 Reed, a date specifically associated with the legend of the Toltec man-god. Cortés stands at the center of the deck wearing the turquoise inlaid mask, the quetzal plume headdress of the god, and a *xicolli* or fringed jacket worn by priests. He is attended by the woman who served as his translator and mistress, Malintzin or Doña Marina, and Pedro de Alvarado who was himself treated as a divinity, the sun god Tonatiuh, because of his red hair.

Why Cortés, a devout Christian, allowed himself to be venerated as the returning pagan god Quetzalcoatl is a mystery. He possibly compared himself to the Renaissance princes who had themselves immortalized in marble or paint as Classical Roman gods. In any case, Cortés' friars would tell him that Quetzalcoatl was no less than the Hercules of the New World. Conquistadors soon learned that there were tremendous political advantages in accommodating such rituals. Stories of returning gods were just one means by which factions in Indian societies could assert their agendas

The *Codex Kingsborough* graphically depicts the horrors that were inflicted on the Aztec Indian people through the *encomienda* system. Here Cortés' agent Anton burns four Indian nobles to death. (Author's illustration)

and legitimize their demands for changes in social and political order. Pizarro was also invoked as the fulfillment of a prophecy of a returning Inca hero named Viracocha. In a remarkable twist on the theme, Spaniards on a later expedition to the Peten jungle of Guatemala were surprised to learn from one Maya lord that the year prophesied for their invasion had not yet arrived and that they should return at a later date or face death. When they did as he advised, they found themselves being used as the pawns in a power struggle between the lord and his rivals all of whom were invoking the prophecies of the sacred calendar to promote themselves into high office.

D: THE MARCH ON TENOCHTITLAN

Battle-worn Spanish troops march out of the Valley of Tlaxcala together with their Indian allies. Despite the myth they propagated of their accomplishments, the fall of Tenochtitlan was not accomplished by a few hundred Conquistadors alone, but by a mighty Indian army numbering in the tens of thousands. In June 1519 Cortés marched out of Cempoala at the head of a confederated army of 300 Spaniards and 250 Totonacs who served as both soldiers and a transport corps to carry the food they would need to live on in enemy territory, as well as an artillery of four falconets. When peace was made with the kingdoms of Tlaxcala a second alliance resulted in the commitment of an initial force of 2,000–3,000 more Indian troops. The Cempoalteca and Tlaxcalteca thereby became the nucleus of an allied army that by 1521 was being led by their own heroic conquerors such as Chichimecatecatl of Tlaxcala and Ixtlilxochitl of Texcoco.

The exact numbers of Indian allies are impossible to determine. Cortés reported that he had 50,000 Tlaxcalteca and that ultimately his Indian army numbered 150,000. His biographer, López de Gómara, spoke of 60,000 troops from Texcoco and 200,000 from Tlaxcala, Huexotzinco, Cholula, and a score of other communities. Whatever the exact figures, the indigenous people, men women and children alike, performed essential logistics work, maintaining the constant supply of weaponry and food upon which any successful campaign ultimately depends, as well as acting as engineers and sappers constructing roads, bridges, cutting timber for ships and other siege machines, and performing demolition.

E: WEAPONS

Steel swords inflicted tremendous damage on Indian armies who had no experience with the metal before their encounters with Europeans. The most basic Conquistador weapon was the medieval-style sword. These were employed both as the 54 in. two-handed variety (1a) and the more common 32 in. form (1b). Later, changing styles in fighting led to the use of fancy hilts with intertwined rings and narrowing blades that would anticipate the rapier (1c). The sword was supported by a very long belt to provide balanced suspension: when the extra length wraps around the body the second time, both hips then support the weight of the sword (1d).

Lances (2) were made of ash wood and ranged in length, but most were probably about 12 ft long. The heads were probably about 8 in., the leaf shape inflicting especially gruesome wounds.

Halberds were generally about 6 ft in length, but could range much longer (3). They consisted of an axe blade with a peak or point opposite it and a long spike or blade on the end. They were adopted from the Swiss who employed halberdiers to exploit breaks in defensive formations of pikemen, but they were ideal for holding Aztec infantry at bay while the gunners and crossbowmen reloaded.

The first matchlocks were a vast improvement over the

Codex Kinsborough shows Luis de Vaca beating two Indian nobles. Vaca was later accused of committing 173 murders. (Author's illustration)

old hand cannon and they were light enough to be held against the gunner's chest and aimed. Heavier versions developed in the 16th century featured a curved stock to help deflect the recoil, perhaps inspiring the term *arquebus* or 'hook gun.' This example is over 4 ft long and employed a lever originally derived from the crossbow for a trigger (4). The barrel could be positioned on a staff for added support.

Crossbows were not only formidable weapons equated with the matchlock in firepower, but they were more dependable in the tropics (5). The stronger composition bows of horn, bone, and wood necessitated the use of a crank or windless (6) to draw back the string. The projectile or 'bolt' (7) was usually about 12 in. long with a short steel head capable of penetrating armor at close range.

The Conquistadors were largely dependent on the falconet for their artillery since there were no wheeled vehicles or beasts of burden capable of hauling the heavier cannon during the opening stages of the invasion (8). The light weight breech loading guns were ordinarily deployed on the rails of ships to repel attackers.

F: ARMOR

To what extent the Conquistadors employed protective armor depended on the campaign and the finances available. They used two types of shields. One, called an *adarga*, was originally of Moorish origin. It was frequently made of heavy ox hide embossed with decorative lines that followed the heart shape of the shield. Most were unpainted (1a). The target was a 2 ft-wide round of wood or metal with hoops on the back through one of which the arm was passed, while the other was grasped by the hand (1b). The convex shape deflected direct thrusts against the body.

Helmets were largely variations on the war hat or *chapel de fer* (2a) which had been easy to produce and provided good protection to the face and neck. The *celata* or *salade* was

equally popular (2b). By the early 16th century the domed *cabasset* (2c) was making its appearance, together with the *burgonet* which was especially popular among officers (2d).

Body armor was very expensive but was crucial to cavalrymen who charged directly into deadly showers of Indian projectiles. The brigandine (3) was a padded linen sleeveless vest to which metal plates about 1 in. wide and 2 in. long were riveted. The plates were usually concealed by a covering of velvet or other fine material, but the rivets were left exposed and were sometimes even gilded. Steel body armor was also available, but was probably limited to the basic including the breast and back plate, tassets for protection of the thighs, and rerebraces and vambraces for the arms (4).

G: CLOTHING

In contrast to the Baroque stereotype of the morion-helmeted captain with the infamous thin goatee beard, most Conquistadors were actually Renaissance men who preferred Italian fashions. By the 1490s the clean-shaven look inspired by Classical art was favored (1a). However, we know that both Indian and Spanish sources all refer to Cortés and his men as having beards, doubtless the result of their being continually engaged in campaign throughout 1519–21. There are many references to their 'flat caps' which could be worn in any variety of forms, but stylish slashes to the brim were favored (1b). By the 1540s short hair and trimmed beards became popular, as well as collared shirts and smaller feather bedecked hats often worn at a jaunty angle over the eye (1c). The shirts were tucked into hose which were tied to a cod piece (2). The hose could then be secured by strings to the upper body garment, either the doublet (3) or the jerkin (4). At times the garments were tailored along such similar lines that it is difficult to distinguish them in contemporary art work. Basically the jerkin was an outer garment worn over the doublet for added protection or warmth. At first such garments featured skirts reaching to the thigh but by the middle of the 16th century fashion trends had shifted to shorter forms.

Footwear was a necessity, but was very hard to come by. High ranking men who also served as the cavalry wore boots (5a). While the foot soldiers doubtless started with a basic leather shoe (5b), they were soon worn out and the men resorted to wearing the indigenous style of sandal (5c).

H: LAST STAND AT THE GREAT TEMPLE, 1521

During the constant skirmishing throughout the summer of 1521, the Spaniards would succeed in making incursions into the center of Tenochtitlan by day only to be driven back out at nightfall. The city itself became a most ingenious form of defense. The streets of Tenochtitlan were maze-like. Once inside, the Spaniards were unable to penetrate without knowing a specific route and they were easily trapped and attacked from all sides and above. The sacred precinct was walled and the temple pyramids contained within them could be manned as refuges or citadels. The Great Temple rose to over 100 feet in height. It had steep sides, staircases, and stepped platforms along which troops could arrange themselves to shower weapons and rocks down on the intruders until such time as they could be relieved from other parts of the city. Here an elite Aztec squadron has gathered in the main plaza to make a defensive stand. A Spanish artillery crew, composed of sailors, are directed to fire their 'lombard' on an assault group charging towards them. Nearby is the giant *tzompantli* or 'skull rack' where the thousands of heads of sacrificial victims from previous Aztec conquests have been displayed.

The irony of victory for Cortés' Indian allies, an illustration from a manuscript preserved in the Glasgow University Library showing Franciscan friars burning the war banners and trophies of the Tlaxcalteca, as well as their sacred idols. (Author's illustration)

I: THE BATTLE OF CAJAMARCA, 1532

Since the days of Columbus, horses had played a fundamental role in all Conquistador expeditions. Indian people generally regarded them as mythical in nature often comparing them to giant deer until they learned their weaknesses. The Aztecs eventually learned to use pikes against them but only very late when the war had already been lost. Learning of Atahualpa's arrival at Cajamarca, Pizarro set a trap for the Inca emperor. First a friar read the *requerimiento*, a 'required' document that outlined the Spaniards' divine rights of conquest. Dismissing it, Atahualpa pointed to the sun and remarked that his own god lived in the heavens, where he looked down upon his own children. In that instant, matchlocks blasted from the doorways where the Spaniards had concealed themselves and with shouts of 'Santiago! Y a ellos!' ('Saint James and at them!'): the cavalry, led by Hernando de Soto, charged directly at Atahualpa's bodyguard with devastating effect. Hooves rang across the courtyard and then thudded against the bare flesh of bodies too tightly packed to flee. Swords rended limbs and lances cut straight through two men at a time. The Inca army was totally surprised and overwhelmed by their first encounter with the horse in warfare. Pizarro himself then charged on foot, cutting his way with sword and dagger to Atahualpa to seize the emperor as his hostage.

J: THE *ENCOMENDERO*, THE *CACIQUE*, AND THE VICAR OF YANHUITLAN

Not all of Mexico was 'conquered.' Many nations were incorporated into the Spanish colonial administration peacefully under the leadership of the indigenous nobility. This scene portrays the Mixtec nobleman Domingo de Guzmán conferring with Vicar Domingo de Santa Maria over a theological issue. The Indian king, or *cacique* as he was called, holds a codex or indigenous book of pictographs in his hands discussing the genealogy of his divine royal ancestors with the friar who holds a bible. Behind them approaches the inquisitive Spanish *encomendero*, Francisco de las Casas. Factional disputes soon emerged over the administration of Indian lands between the Conquistadors, the church, and the Indian nobility. Cortés spent much time in Spain arguing claims to greater titles and more territory, not being satisfied with his appointment as Marqués del Valle de Oaxaca where the Mixtecs and Zapotecs controlled so many rich gold mines.

In Cortés' absence, his son Martín and other relatives were appointed *encomenderos*, which entitled them to extract tribute in free labor. Francisco de las Casas, a cousin, was awarded the encomienda of Yanhuitlan (a rich province) but it was not long before he found himself embroiled in disputes with the Dominican friars over the administration of this kingdom. Although Guzmán, also known as Lord Seven Monkey, was a direct descendant of the epic hero Eight Deer, the *encomendero* felt it was his right to rule as a feudal lord and resented the Dominican's involvement with the cacique. Acting as an effective mediator between the crown and the indigenous nobility who really controlled the land, the church eventually succeeded in forming the more lucrative partnership. By the 17th century the *encomenderos* and their descendants had become largely disenfranchised and their legacy as Conquistadors was forgotten.

INDEX

Figures in **bold** refer to illustrations

COMPANION SERIES FROM OSPREY

ESSENTIAL HISTORIES
Concise studies of the motives, methods and repercussions of human conflict, spanning history from ancient times to the present day. Each volume studies one major war or arena of war, providing an indispensable guide to the fighting itself, the people involved, and its lasting impact on the world around it.

MEN-AT-ARMS
The uniforms, equipment, insignia, history and organization of the world's military forces from earliest times to the present day. Authoritative text and full-color artwork, photographs and diagrams bring over 5000 years of history vividly to life.

ELITE
This series focuses on uniforms, equipment, insignia and unit histories in the same way as Men-at-Arms but in more extended treatments of larger subjects, also including personalities and techniques of warfare.

NEW VANGUARD
The design, development, operation and history of the machinery of warfare through the ages. Photographs, full-color artwork and cutaway drawings support detailed examinations of the most significant mechanical innovations in the history of human conflict.

ORDER OF BATTLE
The greatest battles in history, featuring unit-by-unit examinations of the troops and their movements as well as analysis of the commanders' original objectives and actual achievements. Color maps including a large fold-out base map, organizational diagrams and photographs help the reader to trace the course of the fighting in unprecedented detail.

CAMPAIGN
Accounts of history's greatest conflicts, detailing the command strategies, tactics, movements and actions of the opposing forces throughout the crucial stages of each campaign. Full-color battle scenes, 3-dimensional 'bird's-eye views', photographs and battle maps guide the reader through each engagement from its origins to its conclusion.

AIRCRAFT OF THE ACES
Portraits of the elite pilots of the 20th century's major air campaigns, including unique interviews with surviving aces. Unit listings, scale plans and full-color artwork combine with the best archival photography available to provide a detailed insight into the experience of war in the air.

COMBAT AIRCRAFT
The world's greatest military aircraft and combat units and their crews, examined in detail. Each exploration of the leading technology, men and machines of aviation history is supported by unit listings and other data, artwork, scale plans, and archival photography.

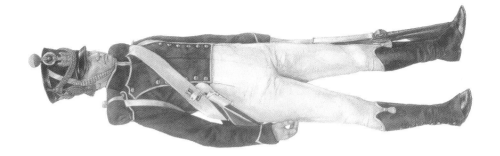

OSPREY PUBLISHING

FIND OUT MORE ABOUT OSPREY

❑ Please send me a FREE trial issue
   of Osprey Military Journal

❑ Please send me the latest listing of Osprey's publications

❑ I would like to subscribe to Osprey's e-mail newsletter

Title/rank _____

Name _____

Address _____

_____

_____

Postcode/zip _____ state/country _____

e-mail _____

Which book did this card come from?

_____

❑ I am interested in military history

My preferred period of military history is _____

❑ I am interested in military aviation

My preferred period of military aviation is _____

I am interested in (please tick all that apply)

❑ general history   ❑ militaria   ❑ model making
❑ wargaming   ❑ re-enactment

Please send to:

USA & Canada: Osprey Direct USA, c/o Motorbooks
International, P.O. Box 1, 729 Prospect Avenue, Osceola,
WI 54020

UK, Europe and rest of world:
Osprey Direct UK, P.O. Box 140, Wellingborough, Northants,
NN8 2FA, United Kingdom

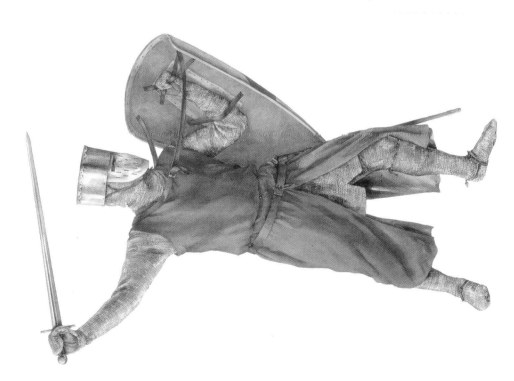

OSPREY
PUBLISHING

www.ospreypublishing.com

call our telephone hotline
for a free information pack

USA & Canada: 1-800-458-0454
UK, Europe and rest of world call:
+44 (0) 1933 443 863

Young Guardsman
Figure taken from *Warrior 22:*
Imperial Guardsman 1799–1815
Published by Osprey
Illustrated by Christa Hook

Knight, c.1190
Figure taken from *Warrior 1: Norman Knight 950 – 1204AD*
Published by Osprey
Illustrated by Christa Hook

POSTCARD